Exercises for the WHOLE BRAIN

Neuron-Builders to Stimulate and Entertain Your Visual, Math and Executive-Planning Skills

by

Allen D. Bragdon

and

Leonard Fellows

Allen D. Bragdon Publishers, Inc.
CAPE COD & SAN FRANCISCO

Allen D. Bragdon Publishers, Inc.
252 Great Western Road
South Yarmouth, MA 02664

An earlier edition of this book was published by
Doubleday & Company as *Diabolical Diversions*.
© 1999 by Allen D. Bragdon Publishers, Inc.
© 1980 by Allen Bragdon and Leonard Fellows
© 1978, 1979 by Allen D. Bragdon
© 1978, 1979 Bragdon/Fellows

BrainWaves® is a registered trademark of
Allen D. Bragdon Publishers, Inc.

Cover design by Cindy Wood.

Library of Congress Catalog Number: 99-90284

ISBN 0-916410-65-X

Printed in the United States of America

00 01 02 03   10 9 8 7 6 5 4 3

INTRODUCTION

"Use it or lose it!" is a catchy phrase that has particular significance for those of us battling to keep our wits about us as we age. Recent research in the cognitive sciences confirms that the stimulation of important centers in the brain will not only dramatically slow the natural decline of one's mental powers but, in fact, help *improve* the function of brain cells. It is also important to understand that the brain's different skills don't compete with each other for space or resources, but rather *support* one another. *E pluribus unum* —"out of many, one" — clearly holds more than one guiding principal for all of us as we go about our daily lives.

The mental exercises in this book are designed to challenge a variety of real-world brain skills in entertaining ways: logical deductive reasoning; creative visualization of forms; manipulation of the symbols and rules of mathematical computation; and application of verbal expression and grammatical logic to identify solutions to problems presented in non-verbal ways. A good illustration of how different skills team together can be found in that cluster of techniques and abilities loosely referred to as *creativity*. Brainstorming is a right-brain activity to the extent that it's non-judgmental, and "divergent" rather than "convergent" in the sense that it's not goal-directed towards a single "right" answer. But in order to produce good results, any brainstorming session must be followed by critical evaluation, to analyze the logical conclusions of each idea, thus sorting the good ones from the bad. Conversely, pushing a simple idea to its logical conclusion may lead to a counterintuitive conclusion, that is sometimes referred to as the "Eureka!" effect.

In like manner, plotting the details of a *Routes* exercise may lead to a flash of insight as the pieces begin to come together. The intuitive visual insight as to a possible solution might pan out after you've applied a detailed analytical check — or it might not!

Number manipulation is a classic left-brain skill, and your left hemisphere will come into play as you work on the *Nimble Numbers* exercises. But many of those puzzles also have visual elements that tap right-brain skills, such as analyzing a collection of numbers both in terms of their abstract mathematical pattern, and their spatial pattern as laid out on the page.

Eye-Ques also present logical conundrums (left brain) in a visual format that may require a contribution from the right-brain's spatial-IQ regions. For most people the "Life or Death Logic" on page 50, for example, requires visualizing the problem in one's mind's eye before determining the answer.

Pat-Turns are the exercises that will tap your right-brain spatial abilities. But again, their complexity will require you to keep track of solutions previously attempted and discarded in a way that will probably call on your left-brain language skills and frontal-lobe planning, organizing, and "mental tracking" abilities.

When visual exercises can be solved with a verbal explanation you'll be able to use left-brain regions to help solve them. Whether you view your linguistic problem-solving faculty as a crutch or invaluable tool depends on your point of view. Different minds work in different ways, and you may find that your approach to solving one of these exercises is different from that of a friend or partner. For that reason, many of these exercises are fun to do in pairs. For a quick test of how different your and your partner's minds really are, try presenting him or her with the "Possible Pairs" exercise on page 48, and then compare your answers. In any case, we believe it's good to have as many problem-solving techniques at your disposal — both individually and collectively — as possible.

A few suggestions:

- We have provided a hint to each answer, printed upside down at the bottom of the page, two pages after the exercise.

- For the faint of heart, we have also supplied a solution to each exercise. It usually can be found upside down five pages after its corresponding exercise. Don't peek and eliminate the challenge!

- You may wish to mark the answers on a separate sheet so you can also challenge a friendly competitor with the problem. If necessary you can make notes on a tissue or clear acetate laid over the page.

- Lay tracing paper over mazes to check your route after you think you have found it by eye alone. To make a maze more challenging, cut a hole the size of a dime in the center of a two-inch-square card. Place the hole at the beginning of a maze and follow the route through the hole as you move the card along the maze paths.

 EYE-QUES: Abstract logic — if A and not B is so, then not-A is not so, but not-B may be so.

 NIMBLE NUMBERS: Number patterns — numbers must obey rules. First figure out the rules that govern a group of numbers.

 PAT-TURNS: Spatial relationships — being forced to visualize a dimension you cannot touch or measure.

 ROUTES: Pathfinding — as in mazes.

CONTENTS

ROUTES

1. THE SWINGING KOALA

When the koala bear pulls on the rope, trace the motion of the pulleys, belts, and pivot rods to figure out whether each weight in the numbered boxes goes up or down. Write your answers next to each numbered box. You engineering types must assume that the koala bear's weight is enough to overcome the friction of all the wheels and weights in the numbered boxes. Nine correct answers, excellent; seven, good; five, fair. There is a hint on the bottom of page 10 and a solution on page 13.

Hint 60
What's the Difference?
Few have been changed
but many omitted
altogether.

6

Solution 59
Swami Swa-You

When you're told "rows 2, 4, and 5," look at the small numbers in the first column at the left. The small numbers next to the first symbol in rows 2, 4, and 5 are 8, 4, and 2. These total 14. Now look for the symbol with number 14 in its lower right-hand corner — it's the star in the circle!

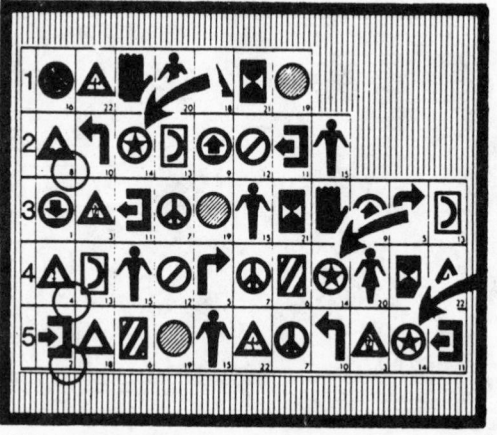

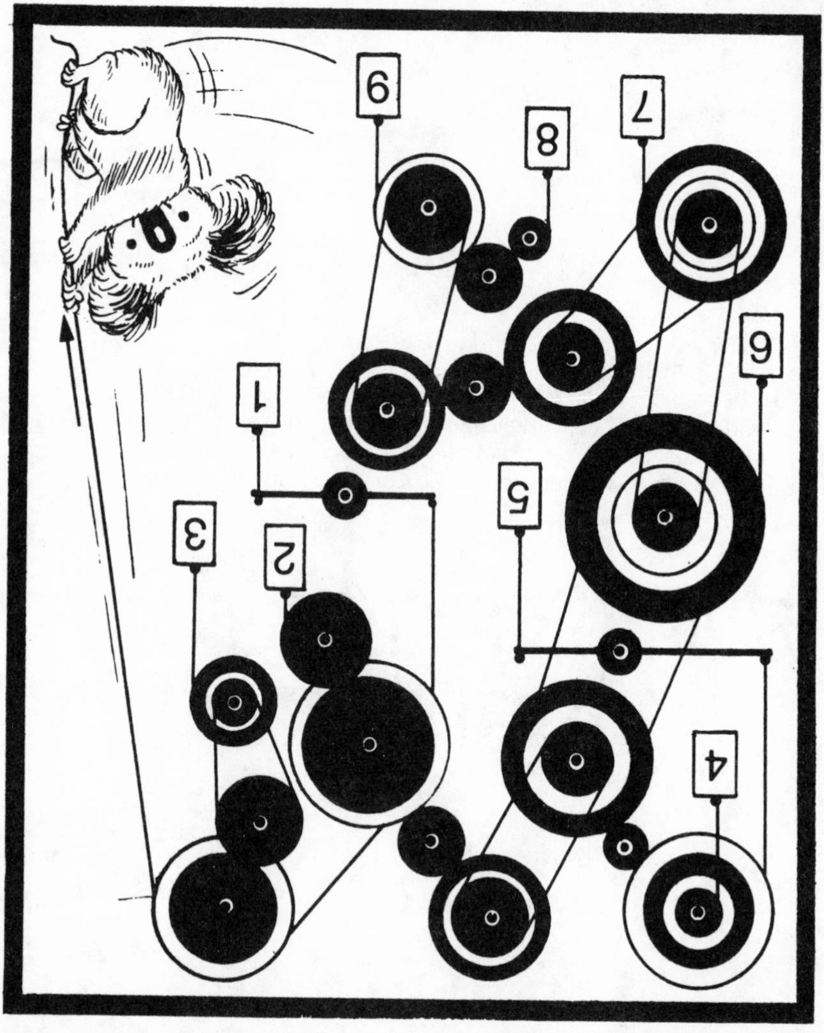

 PAT-TURNS

2. SUMMER REFLECTIONS

The artist wanted to show a summer still life with its exact reflection in a pool, but he made some errors. Can you find ten differences between the top half and its reflection below? Circle the places on each half where you find differences. Par is five minutes. A hint is on the bottom of page 12 and a solution on page 15.

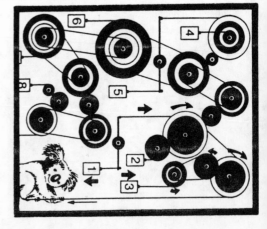

Hint 1
The Swinging Koala

Wheels connected by belts rotate in the same direction. Wheels touching each other rotate in *different* directions. When one end of a bar with a pivot in the middle goes *up*, the other end goes *down*.

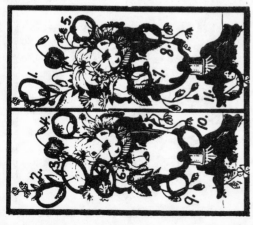

ROUTES

3. KNIGHT FLIGHT

Start at any Kn box and move as a knight moves in chess (over one square and down two or over two and down one) in any direction. You may move only to another dot, and you may pass over dots. You may not land on the same dot twice nor retrace your path as you find your way to the bottom. Your last move must land exactly on a star. To make this more difficult, you can cut a dime-sized hole in the center of a piece of paper (about 3″ × 5″) and lay it over the puzzle so you can see only a few dots at a time as you move it along looking for the correct route. A hint appears at the bottom of page 14 and a solution on page 17.

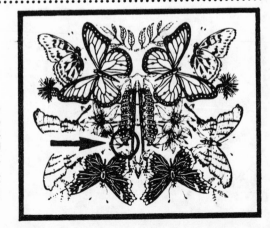

Hint 2
Summer Reflections
The caterpillar in the top
half has an eye, but not
the one in the bottom half.
Can you find nine more
differences?

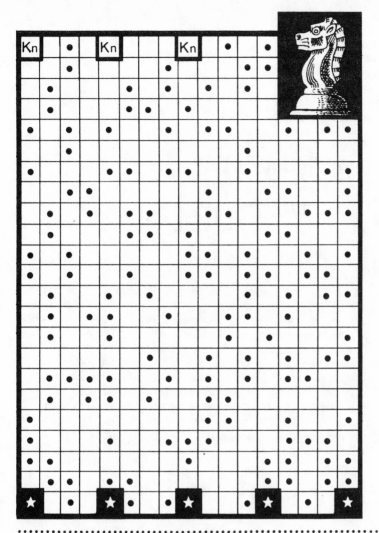

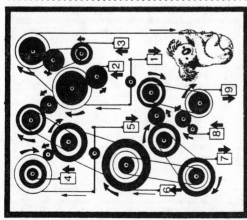

Solution 1
The Swinging Koala

NIMBLE NUMBERS

4. TIMES TABLES

You solve most puzzles by looking for a pattern; then, when you think you've found one, by testing it. Rats find their way through mazes that way. (Sometimes they are also motivated by the smell of food outside the maze they are trapped in.) This puzzle can be solved the same way. (You may also want to promise yourself a reward because, when you figure out the solution, you'll feel so silly you'll need one.) Each of the top three horizontal rows of numbers follows the same mathematical pattern. When you figure out the system, don't ruin it for someone else by filling in the missing number in the bottom row! Time yourself; then see if someone else can solve it faster than you did. There is a hint on page 16 and a solution on page 19.

There is a hint on page 16 and a solution on page 19.

Hint 3
Knight Flight

Three routes have been started. Unfortunately, none is correct. The correct route, which is not shown here, takes twenty-six moves. If you are still stuck, try working back up from the bottom.

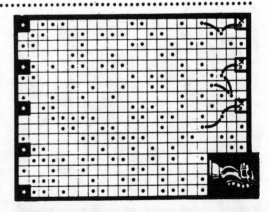

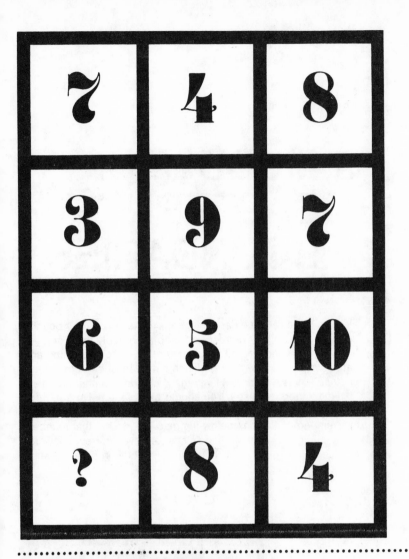

7	4	8
3	9	7
6	5	10
?	8	4

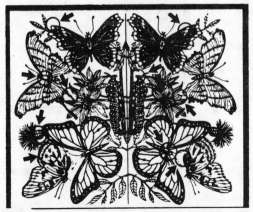

Solution 2
Summer Reflections

ROUTES

5. MUDDLE EASTERN BOUNDARIES

Here are seven Middle Eastern nations in the news. Their boundary conflicts can quickly be resolved by drawing only three sraight lines from any side of the box to any other without touching any nation. When you are through, each nation must be completely enclosed in its own area. Henry-the-K couldn't do it in three years, so Jimmy tried it himself. You should be able to solve it in three minutes. Write the name of each of the seven nations next to one of the numbers in the box below the map. Then write that number in the circle next to that nation's shape. Seven correct answers, excellent; five, good; four, fair. There is a hint on page 18 and a solution on page 21.

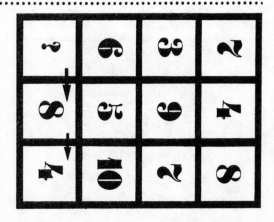

Hint 4
Times Tables

If you do your figures from east to west, multiply your efforts and subtract the rest. You'll find the solution and pass the test.

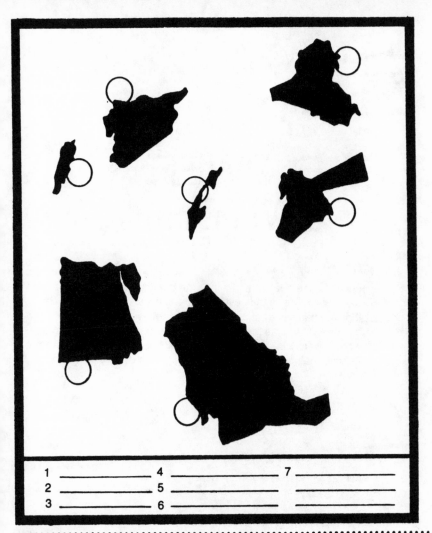

1 _____ 4 _____ 7 _____
2 _____ 5 _____
3 _____ 6 _____

Solution 3
Knight Flight

Hint 5
Muddle Eastern
Boundaries

Lebanon, the small one on the far left, and Israel, the small one in the center, are enclosed by the smallest triangle. The first line you draw should divide Saudi Arabia and Egypt and fence Syria off from Iraq.

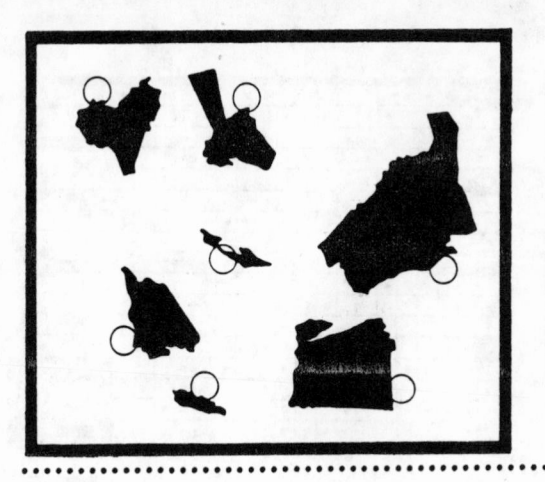

EYE-QUES

6. FLOWER SWITCH

Here are three boxes of flowers, one containing one dozen roses, one with one dozen carnations, and a third with six roses and six carnations. But all the covers have been switched. Now, imagine that you can select one box. Shut your eyes, open the box, take out a flower, and close the cover. When you open your eyes and see what flower you have, can you tell which flowers are in each box? Par is three minutes. A hint is on page 20 and a solution is on page 23.

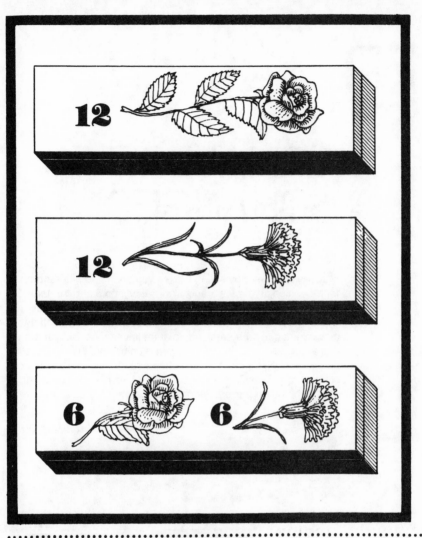

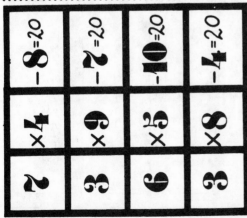

7. SMALL CHANGES

Try this one on the guy sitting next to you on the commuter train. Place pennies on circles 3 and 8 and dimes on 5 and 10. By moving the coins one at a time in straight lines, only along the dotted lines, make the pennies and dimes switch places. No two coins can occupy the same circle at the same time, but you can jump empty spaces. You can move the coins one, two, or three spaces, but you cannot pass a space already occupied. An expert coinman can do this one in ten moves or fewer. Can you beat that? A hint appears on page 22 and a solution on page 25.

Hint 6
Flower Switch
Start with the box whose cover gives you the most information.

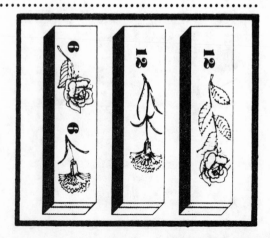

Solution 5
Muddle Eastern
Boundaries

1. Saudi Arabia
2. Syria 3. Lebanon
4. Iraq 5. Jordon
6. Israel
7. United Arab
   Republic

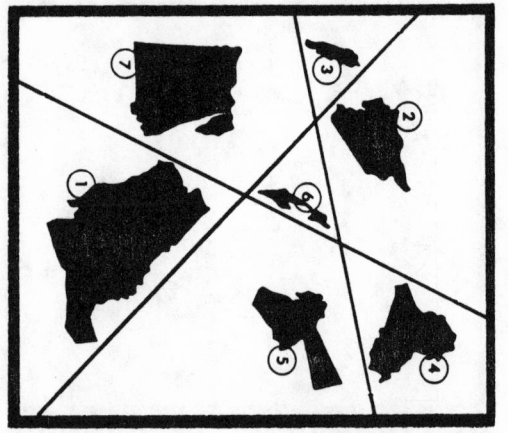

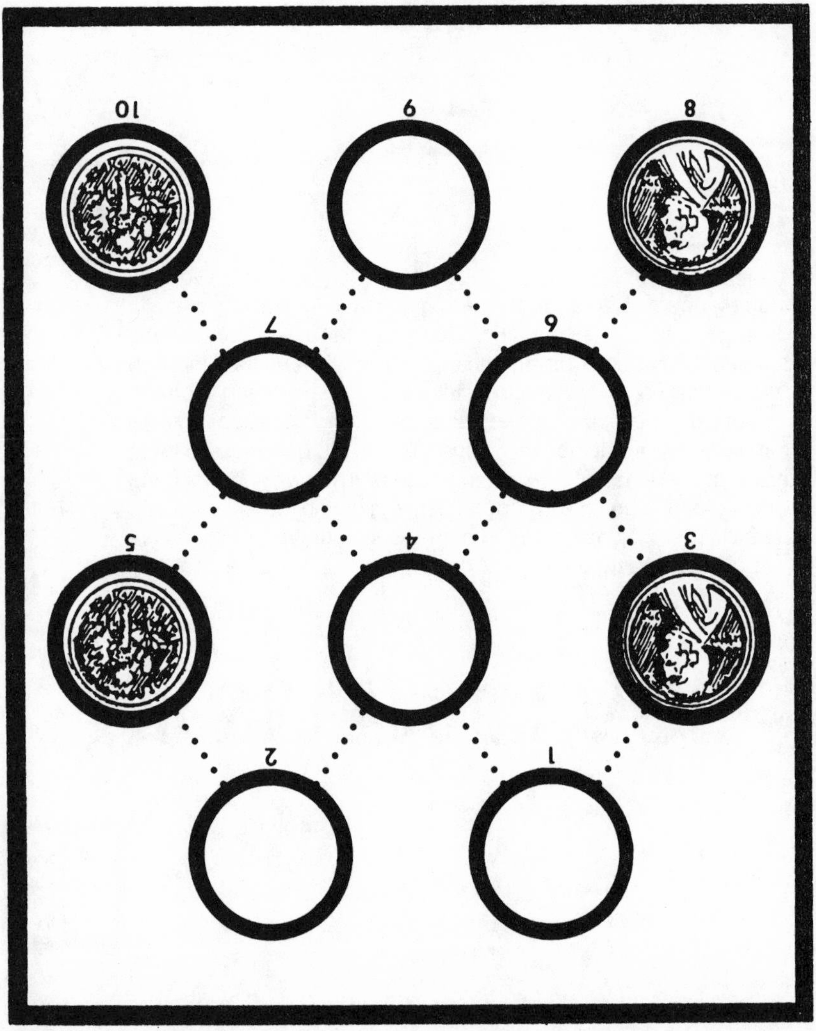

NIMBLE NUMBERS

8. MATH CLASS

The teacher wrote four math problems on the blackboard and asked four students to answer them. The students' responses are shown in the boxes next to their heads. The teacher said, "Your math is pretty bad! Three of you have two correct answers and one of you didn't even get *one* correct!" Can you figure out which are the right answers, which students had two, and who had *none* correct? The small numbers in the boxes are the numbers of the questions the teacher asked; the large numbers are the students' answers to those questions. Time: one minute, excellent; three minutes, good; five minutes, fair. A hint appears on page 24 and a solution on page 27.

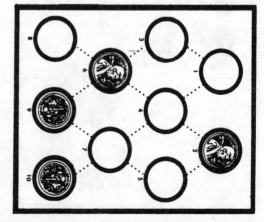

Hint 7
Small Changes
Move the coin in circle 8 to circle 2, then the penny in circle 3 to circle 6. Then move the dime from 5 to 9.

Solution 6
Flower Switch

Select the box with the cover marked "six and six." If you blind-picked a rose, a dozen roses must be in that box (because the covers were switched). The box with the "twelve roses" cover must contain twelve carnations. The carnation box, therefore, contains the six carnations and six roses. If, on the other hand, you blind-picked a carnation from the box marked "six and six," a dozen carnations must be in that box, the dozen roses in the "twelve carnations" box, and the carnations and roses in the rose box.

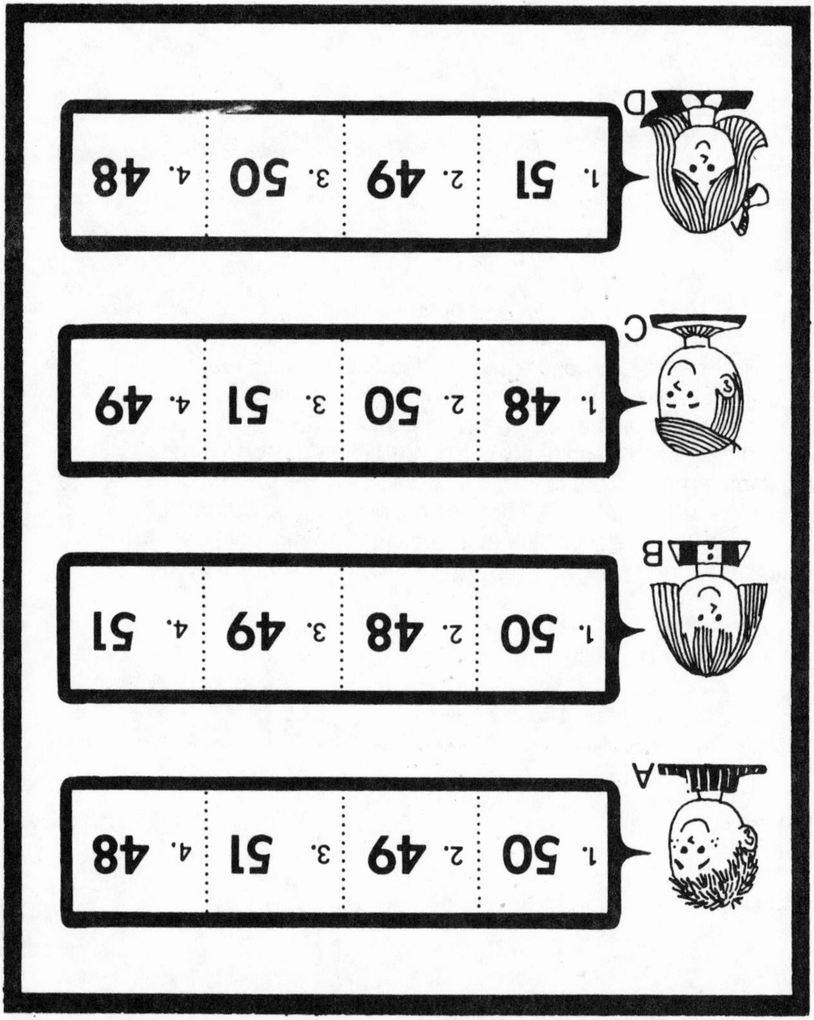

NIMBLE NUMBERS

9. TIME PIECES

Sir Rodney Koala has found a replica of the great stone clock that graced the archway at the entrance to the ancient town of Caesareo in Italy. During the uprising of 1733, a near-miss by a bomb caused severe cracks in the face of the clock. The cracks happened to separate the face into four pieces, each having roman numerals that added up to 20. The sample shown is a forgery because each section totals a different number. Can you find where the cracks appeared on the original? Par is six minutes to find at least one of the multiple possibilities. A hint appears on page 26 and a solution on page 29.

A hint appears on page 26 and a solution on page 29.

Hint 8
Math Class

Two of the students, A and B, answered the first question correctly. One of those two also answered the second question correctly; the other got the third question right. Now, if you can't figure out the correct answer to all four questions, keep away from logic problems.

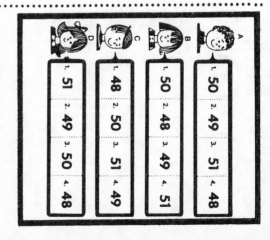

"The time?
It's exactly VIII : XXVII."
21
20
19
18

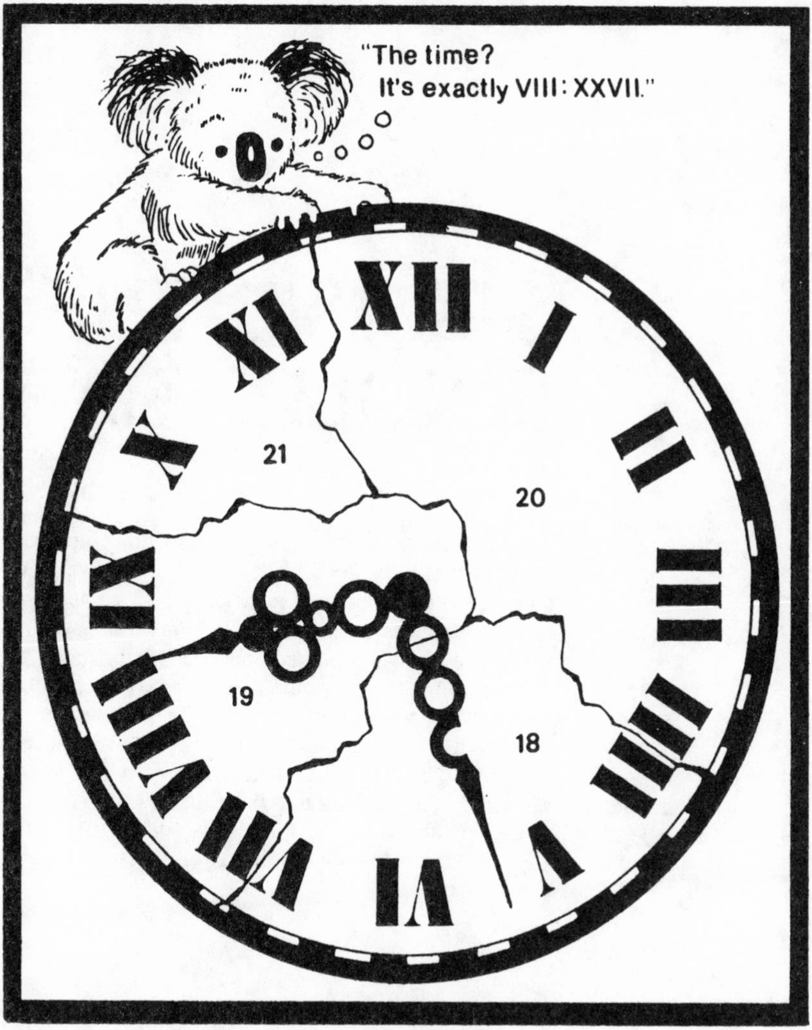

Solution 7
Small Changes

Move the coin in circle 8 to circle 2, then 3 to 6, 5 to 9, 10 to 1, 2 to 5, 6 to 4, 9 to 6, 1 to 3, 4 to 10 and, finally, 6 to 8.

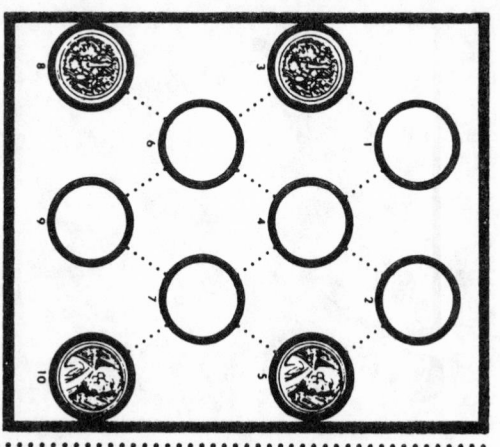

 EYE-QUES

10. SIX AND THE SINGLES BAR

Have you ever wondered why some perfectly delightful, otherwise "normal" people prefer to live alone all their lives, *or* why so many objects in nature are paired, like ears and nostrils? Then have you ever wondered why you wondered about that? Why the most common practice is automatically assumed to be the best? Or how much duller life would be if it had *no* choices in it that people could make for themselves? The puzzle on the opposite page is very "normal." There are two of almost all the objects. What makes it interesting is the "almost." It should not take you more than four minutes to pick out the few objects that there are only one of — unless, of course, you are *so* normal the idea is unthinkable. A hint appears on page 28 and a solution on page 31.

Hint 9
Time Pieces

Sir Rodney found one section of the clock under his table at a caffè where he stopped for a cappuccino. Finding the others is up to you.

Solution 8
Math Class

The four correct answers were:
Question 1 — 50;
Question 2 — 48;
Question 3 — 51;
Question 4 — 49.
A had Question 1 (50)
  and Question 3 (51) correct.
B had Question 1 (50)
  and Question 2 (48) correct.
C had Question 3 (51)
  and Question 4 (49) correct.
D had none correct.

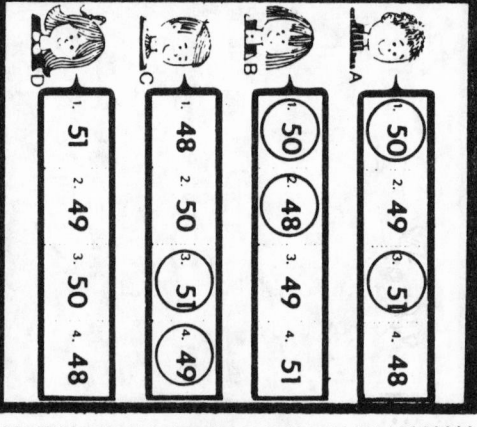

 NIMBLE NUMBERS

11. LOVER'S LABOR'S LOST

The princess was in tears. Her father had set a challenge for her handsome, dumb, and therefore most desirable suitor. The king spoke: "You may have the hand of my daughter only if you are able to divide this map of the numbered counties in my kingdom (opposite page) into four identical provinces. Each province must have the same shape and area, and each must contain county numbers totaling exactly 45." The sly princess then innocently remarked to her slack-jawed lover, "Isn't it an interesting fact that the sum of the numbers from 1 to 9 totals exactly 45?" The young man never did figure out the solution so the princess married a frog who solved it in one minute nineteen seconds. Are you as smart as a frog? A hint appears on page 30 and a solution on page 33.

Hint 10
Six and the Singles Bar
Look for warm-blooded
animals and the tea that is
most pleasing to the
palate.

28

Solution 9
Time Pieces

According to a puzzle
authority, there are thirteen
ways to accomplish this.
Here is one. How many
more can you figure out?

EYE-QUES

12. SWEET LOGIC

Study the cakes shown in the top two horizontal rows. After you figure out the pattern for these rows, find the numbered cake (1 through 6) in the box at the bottom that would complete the third row in the top box. Score yourself: fifteen seconds, you take the cake; one minute, try blowing out the candles instead; five minutes, better ask someone to cut your serving of cake into bite-sized pieces for you. A small hint appears on page 32 and a solution on page 35.

Hint 11
Lover's LaBor's Lost
Each province contains every number from 1 through 9. The lines drawn here are the beginning of a correct partitioning.

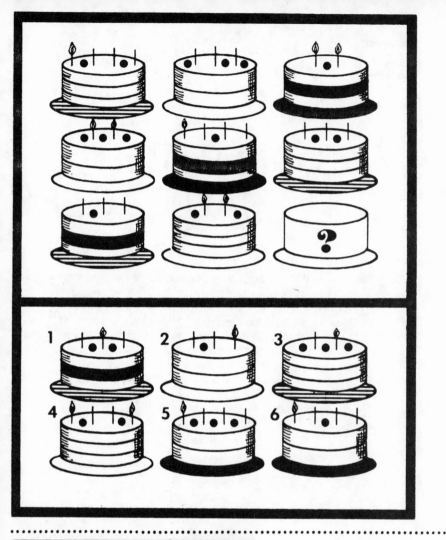

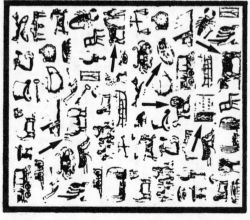

Solution 10
Six and the
Singles Bar

1. Jockey and horse
2. Sheep
3. Box of tea
4. Bull
5. Artist's palette
6. Lion

13. SMARTER THAN EAGLES

Pretend that you are a not-so-hungry eagle hovering over the ruins of a Mayan temple deep in the jungles of Mexico. You have spotted a plump jaguar cub and have made this silent deal with him: "Little cat, if you can run from where you are now (X) to the holy chamber (Y) and pass through every open slot between the buildings without once retracing your path, I will *not* swoop down and tear you apart with my fierce beak and razor-sharp talons." Now, pretend you are the cub. You have 120 seconds in which to insure that you will be able to grow up to eat eagles! A hint appears on page 34 and a solution on page 37.

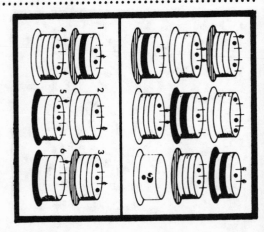

Hint 12
Sweet Logic
The *position* of the candles and cherries doesn't matter.

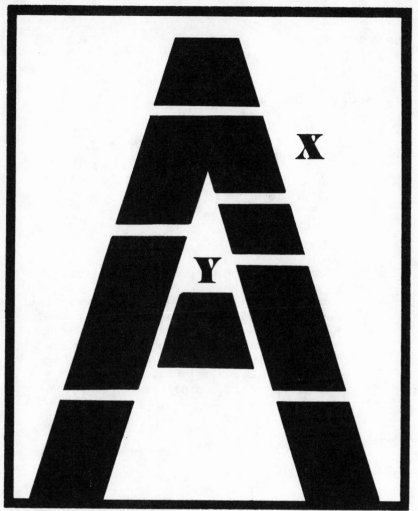

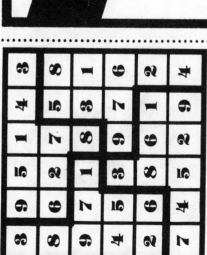

PAT-TURNS

14. ICON, CAN YOU?

A Christian martyr working by candlelight deep in the grotto of the Cumaean Sibyl had spent all his life trying in vain to restore this ancient relic by correctly positioning the eight pieces that had been cut from it with diabolical precision by ravaging invaders. Finally, he arranged them as you see them here before the feet of the wise and ancient sibyl. Then, with his dying breath, he begged her help. She did it in forty-three seconds — with her toes! Write the number of each piece in the circle where it belongs. A hint is on page 36 and a solution on page 39.

Hint 13
Smarter than Eagles

The young cub was tempted to dart directly in between the first two buildings, but, though he was more exposed to the hovering eagle, he started his route correctly around the *top* of the ruins.

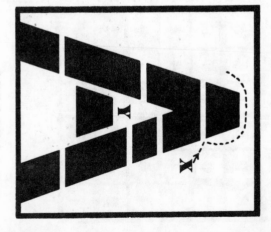

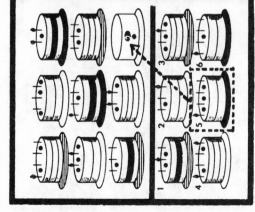

Solution 12
Sweet Logic

Number 5 completes the third row. Each row has (a) one of each type plate; (b) one cake with two white layers, one with three white layers, and one with two white and one black layer; (c) two, three, and four candles; (d) one and two lighted candles; and (e) one, two, and three cherries.

NIMBLE NUMBERS

15. HOT SHOTS

These moving targets may be tough to hit, but we're sure you can cop a Kewpie doll in seven shots. Hit the two correct targets in each row and at the end make sure your seventh shot hits the gong. When the math is done as directed after each hit, the total score, including the gong, must be 225 — exactly 225. If it takes you longer than five minutes or more than seven shots, go buy some cotton candy and come back to try again! If you want a Kewpie doll badly enough to need a hint, look on page 38. A solution appears on page 41.

Hint 14
Icon, Can You?

The numbered pieces to be placed in the picture are not necessarily right side up, as shown in this puzzle. Start by placing numbers 1 and 3 as indicated here.

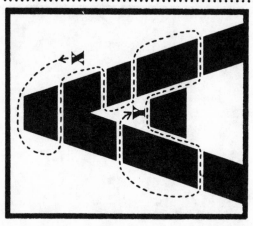

Solution 13
Smarter than Eagles

ROUTES

16. ARF RIGHT

These four dogs — the Afghan hound (A), the dachshund (B), the Pekingese (C), and the poodle (D) — are commonly thought to have originated in the four countries whose shapes are shown here. In fact, two of the dogs actually originated in the same country. First name each country. Then put the letter in each box for the dog that is commonly thought to have originated in that country. Finally, draw a continuous line from each dog to its country without crossing any other dog's line. (The dogs don't fight, but the countries tend to.) Par is four and a half minutes. Some hints appear on page 40 and a solution on page 43.

Hint 15
Hot Shots
Work your way down, hitting two targets in each row before you reach the next one.

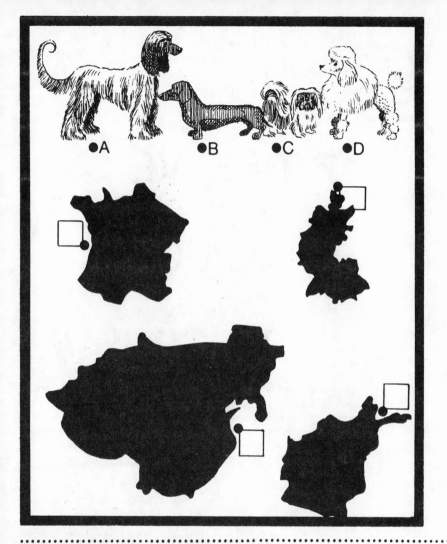

Solution 14
Icon, Can You?

NIMBLE NUMBERS

17. TWELVE WAYS TO BE UNLUCKY

Here are nine number-cards that got mixed up during a brawl at the Sunday-night bingo table run by the Golden Years Club. To straighten them out again for the old folks, switch the cards around so that each of the six horizontal rows of numbers (in boxes) and each of the six vertical columns of numbers (outside boxes, on their sides) total 13. Some cards may also have to be rotated. This puzzle is a lot easier to do if you cut out each of the nine squares and rearrange them until you get it. But if you don't want to cut up this book, see the hint on page 42. Par (without cutting out the squares) is ten minutes. A solution appears on page 45.

● ●

Hint 16
Arf Right

A is for Afghanistan, B is for Berlin, C is for Chairman Mao, and therefore D is for . . . ? One of the big dogs comes from one of the smallest countries. We're pretending the poodle comes from France. And we know the capital of China is Peking

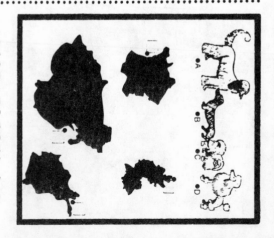

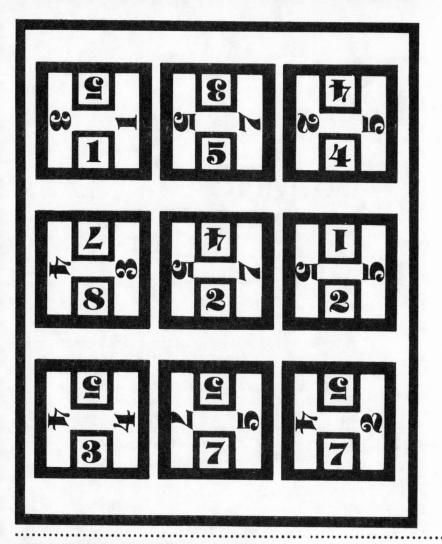

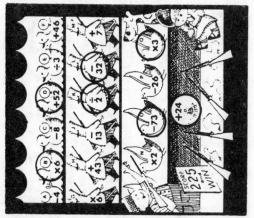

Solution 1
Hot Shots

Top row
+52×6=312
Second row
312−32=280÷2=140
Bottom row
140−73=67×3=201
Gong
201+24=225

PAT-TURNS

18. MRS. PRITCHETT'S PIQUE

When her married daughter wasn't looking, Mrs. Pritchett — in a fit of pique because she had not been invited to her daughter's bridge party — changed her daughter's flower arrangement so that all the black centers would line up on four straight lines, with three centers in each line. She did it in ninety seconds and moved only two flowers before her daughter turned around. She didn't even notice, which made her mother even madder. Can you duplicate Mrs. Pritchett's feat? A hint appears on page 44 and a solution on page 47.

A hint appears on page 44 and a solution on page 47.

Hint 17
Twelve Ways
to Be Unlucky
We've shown you how to reassemble the cards in the top row. Now you put the rest in their proper places and turn them all right side up.

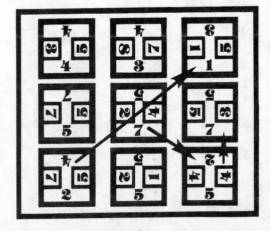

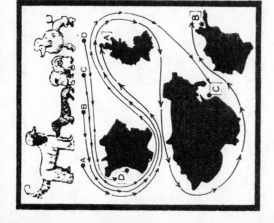

43

PAT-TURNS

19. TWISTING BLOCKS

All of these blocks are identical. By studying them, can you answer the following questions? First, imagine that block A will be placed on top of this stack so the number 1 is right side up on the side where the arrow is pointing. What number will be on the bottom of A?

What number will be on:

... the right side of B?___.

... the bottom of C?___.

... the top of D?___.

... the bottom of E?___.

What numbers are on the bottoms of F___, G___, H___?

Eight correct answers, excellent; five, good; three, fair. A hint is on page 46 and a solution appears on page 49.

Hint 18
Mrs. Pritchett's Pique

We have shown you one move here. If we showed you the other, this wouldn't be a hint, it would be a solution. (That appears on page 105.)

44

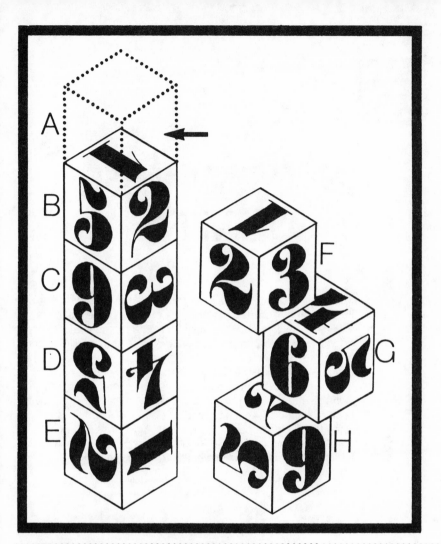

A
B
C
D
E

F
G
H

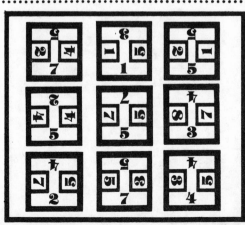

Solution 17
Twelve Ways
to Be Unlucky

45

NIMBLE NUMBERS

20. DOMI-YES, DOMINO

The game of dominoes was the greatest of the three passions indulged in by Czarist generals. (The other two were played out with mere soldiers and/or women.) Imagine two generals, during a lull in the Crimean campaign, hunched huge and bearlike in their greatcoats over ten dominoes laid out on a campaign chest. Their eyebrows are already dripping icicles as the winter night deepens and the snow drifts around their boots. They ponder this problem: "When the correct number of dots are put on the blank dominoes, each of the rows (two across and one down) will add up to the same total." Please put in the dots for the generals and get the four correct numbers before the Bolsheviks come. They only have about sixty years left. A hint appears on page 48 and a solution on page 51.

• •

Hint 19
Twisting Blocks

We have written in the numbers on block A, in their correct positions. Obviously, the number on the bottom of block A cannot be either a 1 or a 2 or a 3. If you look at block B, you can see that a 5 is next to the 2, not opposite it. So that leaves the 4 or the 6. It's the 4. Look at the others; you will see why.

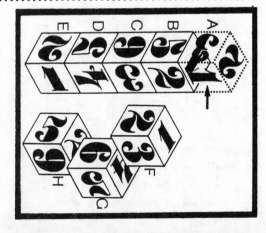

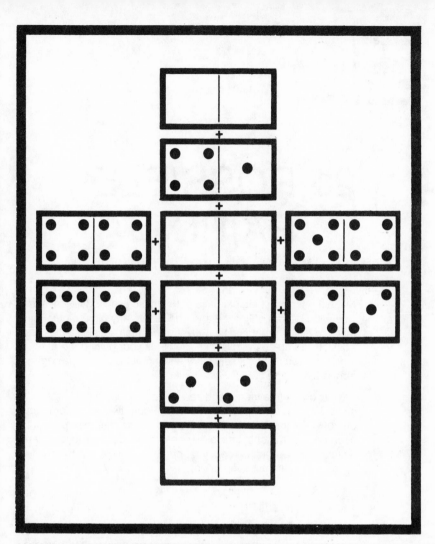

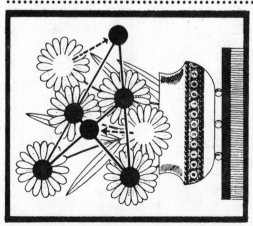

21.POSSIBLE PAIRS

Make the ten most logical pairs out of these twenty different items. Use each picture only once and don't leave any picture out. Pair them so all ten are the *most likely* combinations of similarities. One possible set of ten pairs is on page 50. Is your pairing more logical? If you think so, see if it beats another possible pairing that appears on page 53.

Try this one with a friend, and see if you can match the items in the same way you think your friend would. Score two points for each pair of yours that matches your friend's answer and one point for each pair not matching his or her answer; if you *have* to leave any picture out, subtract one point for each. Par: sixteen to twenty, like minds; ten to fifteen, keep talking; five to ten, way out!

Hint 20
Domi-Yes, Domino
One square in the bottom domino is blank and the top domino has two bullet holes in it.

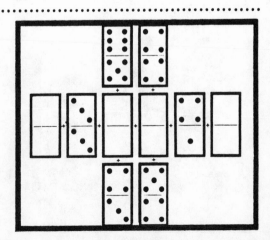

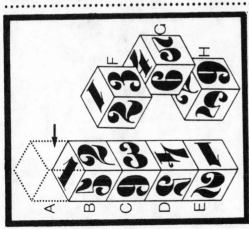

Solution 19
Twisting Blocks

A—4, B—3, C—4,
D—6, E—3, F—6,
G—2, H—4

EYE-QUES

22. LIFE-OR-DEATH LOGIC

Anders Andert Andersen is off to an outpost in Alaska that is a six-day hike from Shungnak across a desolate expanse of snow and ice. One man can lug only sufficient food and water for four days. As you can see, one man can't go alone because his supplies wouldn't last until he reached his destination. How many people would it take carrying supplies to assure that Anders reaches the outpost and his assistants make it back to Shungnak? Par is ten minutes. There's a hint on page 52, and our answer is on page 55.

Hint 21
Possible Pairs
(One Possibility)

flower — bee
carved bust — chisel
bell buoy — ship
milk — glass
cow — butter
watering can — saltshaker
marine signal flags — music
hatchet — tree
oak leaf — acorn
knife — bread

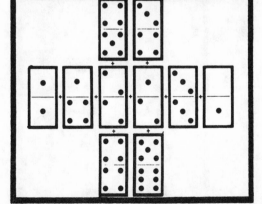

Solution 20
Domi-Yes, Domino

ROUTES

23. A JOG THROUGH THE PARK

This early-morning jogger doesn't know it yet, but he is going to be late for work. Can you find the path that will bring him back out where he started? Some paths stop altogether; some pass under or over others. You might want to really challenge yourself. Cut a dime-sized hole out of the center of a piece of paper about two inches square. Try to find the correct route by sliding the paper along and looking at the path through the hole only. Par: Under two minutes. A hint appears on page 54. A solution is on page 57.

· ·

Hint 22
Life-or-Death Logic
No matter how many people start out at Shungnak, only Anders has to arrive at the outpost. But remember: even assistants need to eat, so make sure the others have enough food and water to get them home.

52

Solution 21
Possible Pairs
(Another Possibility)

carved bust — music
bell buoy — marine signal
   flags
ship — glass
milk — cow
butter — saltshaker
knife — bread
acorn — tree
leaf — watering can
hatchet — chisel
bee — flower

EYE-QUES

24. WHAT IN THE WORLD?

What does this drawing show? Choose from A, B, C, or D, below:

A. Layout of a new petroleum refinery proposed by Royal Dutch Shell for the Saudi Arabian port of Jiddah.
B. Artist's rendering of the diesel prewarmer for the stage-one rocket of the NASA Thor space exploration vehicle.
C. Diagrammatic of the fuel system of a BMW 530i automobile.
D. Schematic for the seawater purification and distillation plant on the cruise ship S.S. *Statendam*.

If you think you *really* know your engineering, try matching the numbers in the drawing to this list of components:

Fuel tank	Pump	Pressure regulator
Ring line	Charcoal filter	Filter
Collector	Starting valve	Injection valve
Suction device	Reservoir	Expansion tank

A hint appears on page 56. The solution is on page 59.

Hint 23
A Jog Through the Park

Some people find it easier to solve mazes by starting from the exit and working toward the entrance.

Solution 22
Life-or-Death Logic

It would take three travellers. One assistant carries four day's supplies, and after the first day's trek, he gives one day's supplies to the other assistant and one to Anders. This gives them full four-day packs again. The first assistant, with his day's supply remaining, then returns home. The other two complete another day's trip, at the end of which the other assistant gives one day's supplies to Anders who again has four day's supplies, sufficient to reach the outpost. His assistant still has enough to reach home in two days.

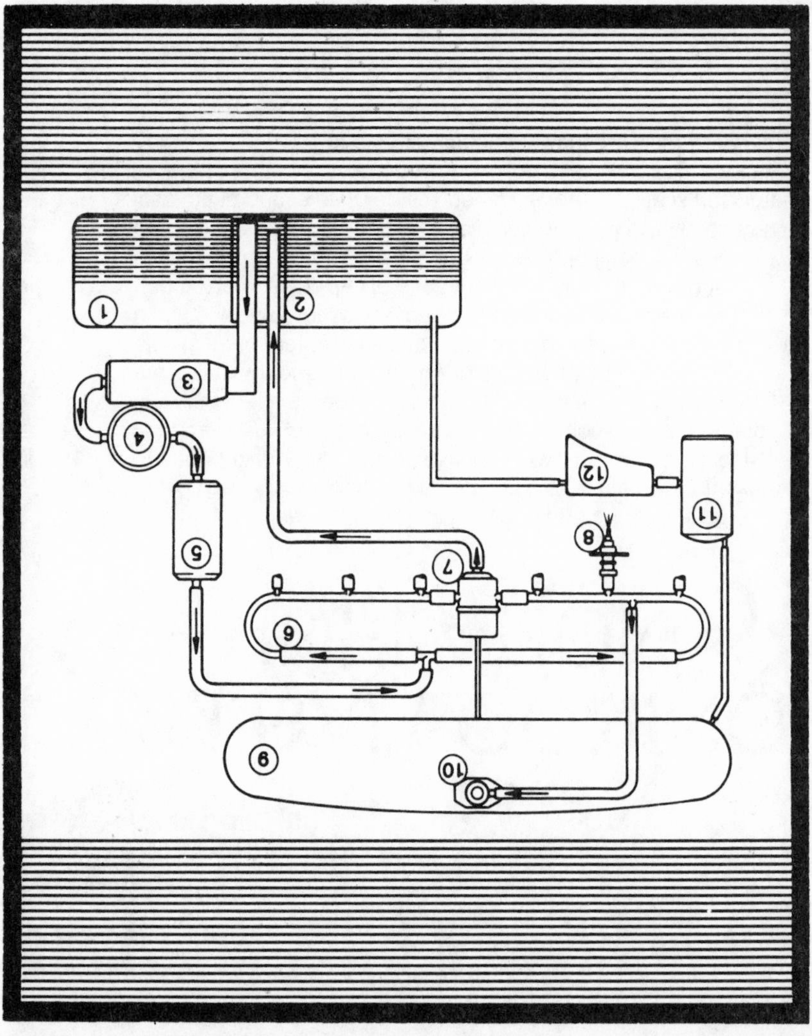

NIMBLE NUMBERS

25. BALLOONING INFLATION

In a picturesque, old ministate located north of Cuba and southwest of Nova Scotia, inflation is so bad that prices have to be changed every few minutes to keep up with it. So the balloon vendors there write the prices on their balloons in the morning, knowing that if a balloon is worth one koch early in the morning, it must be sold for fifteen koches in the late afternoon. They have also learned that twice as many people buy white balloons as buy black ones. For these reasons it has become the custom at the beginning of each day to price the day's stock of balloons consecutively (in this case, from one koch to fifteen) in such a way that the prices on all the white balloons will total exactly double the total of the prices on the black ones. As you see, life is not simple for a small businessman there. Can you give this kindly, Old-World gentleman a hand pricing his fifteen balloons? A hint appears on page 58 and a solution on page 61.

• •

Hint 24
What in the World?

Come on now, what set of plans is a couple of ordinary puzzle makers most likely to have access to? And don't you agree that the fuel tank looks like an automobile grille?

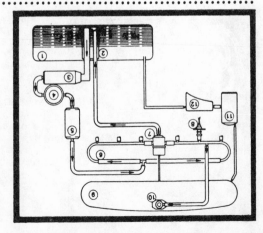

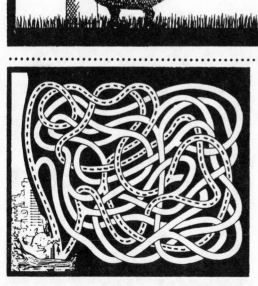

Solution 23
A Jog Through
the Park

ROUTES

26. MAGIC QUILT

There are six different symbols in this quilt. If you can pick the three magic symbols to work with, you can jump from one to another in a continuous path from the top row to the bottom. Your path must move through all three magic symbols you picked — though not necessarily in the same order each time — before you move to any one of them again. Your path may go up or down vertically or across horizontally, but may never go diagonally. Can you find the three magic symbols and their route from the top to the bottom? A hint appears on page 60 and a solution on page 63.

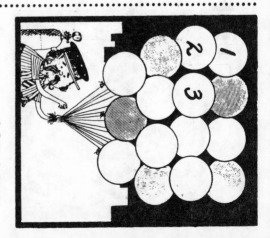

Hint 25
Ballooning Inflation

The five numbers on the black balloons are consecutive and add up to exactly 40.

Solution 24
What in the World?

Diagrammatic of the fuel system in a BMW 530i automobile.
1. Fuel tank   2. Suction
3. Pump   device
4. Expansion tank
5. Filter   6. Ring line
7. Pressure regulator
8. Injection valve
9. Collector 10. Starting valve
11. Charcoal filter
12. Reservoir

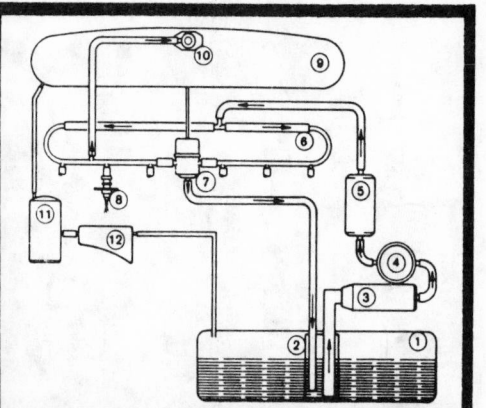

PAT-TURNS

27. OPEN AND SHUT CASES

The koala bear who calls himself "Sir Rodney" has gone a little gaga from smoking eucalyptus leaves. Though he constructed this wondrous contraption for opening and closing the doors of his friends' cages, he cannot recall any longer which doors open and which close when he turns the crank handle clockwise. Fortunately, all the animals enjoy surprises, so they don't really care. If you have an orderly mind, feel free to follow the cogged gears, belted wheels, and elliptical gears to the pulleys connected to the cage doors — then predict whether the doors will open or close for the (1) toucan, (2) monk, (3) hare. A hint appears on page 62 and a solution on page 65.

Hint 26
Magic Quilt
Triangle, stripes, and a
Sign four-square.
Will lead you truly
From here to there.

60

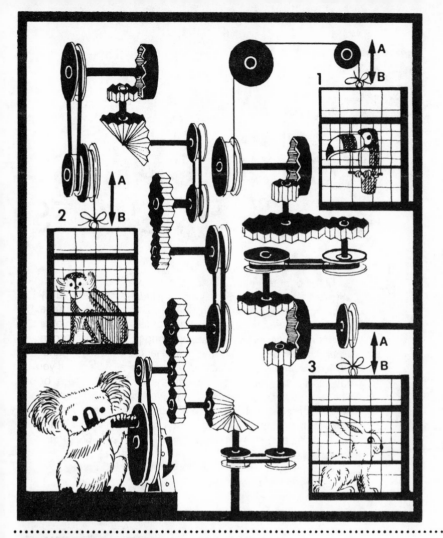

Solution 25
Ballooning Inflation

61

NIMBLE NUMBERS

28. DIPLOMATS' DILEMMA

Six of the brightest students at a school for diplomats' children were told there were fewer than sixty pennies in this bank, but not even the teacher knew exactly how many, so they must guess by weighing it. When the teacher wasn't looking, one child shook all the coins out, counted them exactly, and put them back. They agreed that they all would give answers that were too high or too low (shown in the boxes) so she wouldn't know which one had done it. But they did tell her they all knew the answer and that one of their answers was nine off, one four off, and the others, six, one, twelve, and eleven off. If she could guess the correct number of pennies, they said, she would know who had counted them because his or her answer was closest to correct. (Being good diplomats they also made her agree either not to punish them at all or to punish all of them equally if she did guess correctly.) Who did it and what is the correct answer? A hint appears on page 64 and a solution on page 67.

....

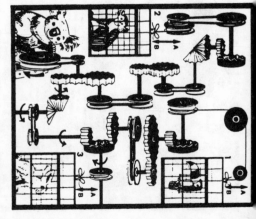

Hint 27
Open and Shut Cases

Elliptical gears (the cone-shaped ones at right angles to each other) rotate in *opposite* directions. Therefore if one turns clockwise, it will push the other counterclockwise, and *vice versa.*

PAT-TURNS

29. MENTAL JIGSAW

This is a reproduction of a Nootka Eskimo wood carving showing a lightning snake, a wolf, a thunderbird, and a killer whale. Write the number of each piece that has been cut out of the picture in the circle where that piece should go. Nine correct answers, excellent; seven, good; five, fair. Turn to page 66 if you want some hints to get you going. A solution appears on page 69.

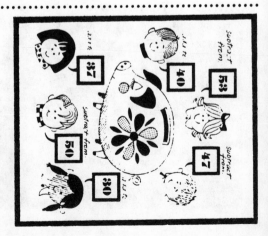

Hint 28
Diplomats' Dilemma
Half the answers are too high. Since the correct answer is under sixty, try subtracting the largest amount from the highest answer.

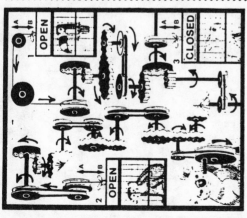

PAT-TURNS

30. CUBISTICS

While he was ambling pensively through the forest one spring day,
Sir Rodney Koala found a beautiful piece of unblemished
eucalyptus bark from which he decided to cut out a form which
could be folded to make a big wooden block (hollow, of course).
He then put letters from the koalese alphabet on each side of the
finished block. How many and which of the seven numbered cubes
shown could *not* have been formed from Sir Rodney's pattern? A
hint appears on page 68 and a solution on page 71.

A hint appears on page 68 and a solution on page 71.

Hint 29
Mental Jigsaw

The pieces are not always
shown right side up. Three
pieces have been put into
their correct spots for you.

Solution 28
Diplomats' Dilemma

The little boy from Baghdad who said "forty" is the culprit because the correct answer is forty-one. It works this way:
53−12, 50−9, 47−6, 30+11, 37+4, 40+1.

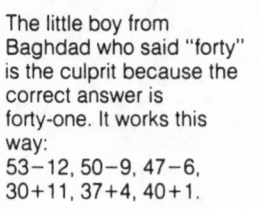

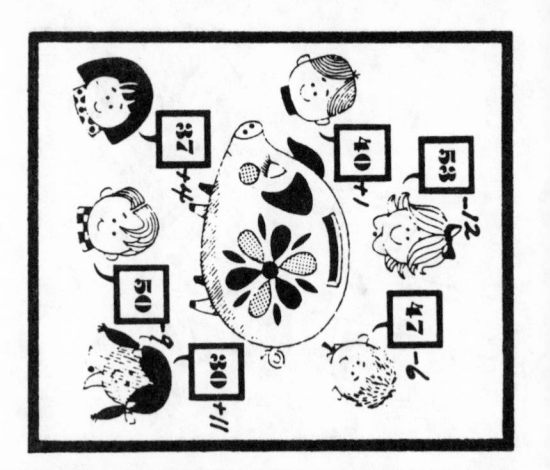

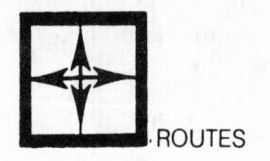

31. SNOW FAKES

The little box with the three symbols and the numbers 1, 2, and 3 shows the points scored for passing each symbol in this maze. Figure out the route from box A to box B which collects the *fewest* number of points. Some folks can amass as few as forty points. Can you beat that? A hint appears on page 70 and a solution that beats the forty-point barrier on page 73.

Hint 30
Cubistics

If you can't fold the sample cube with your mind's fingers and rotate it in your mind's eye, try *unfolding* the others. Notice which end of a letter faces which side of another letter — the open side of the C and the H, for example.

★ = 1   ● = 2   ✳ = 3

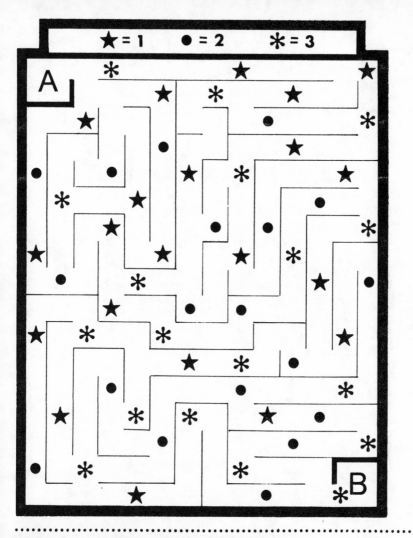

Solution 29
Mental Jigsaw

A—7, B—5, C—3,
D—9, E—1, F—6,
G—2, H—8, J—4

NIMBLE NUMBERS

32. TAG SALE

For your birthday you have been given $100 by an eccentric uncle to spend at a local church tag sale, but your purchases must total exactly $100. You may buy more than one of any item. Which items in what quantities would you have to buy? Par is two minutes. A hint appears on page 72 and a solution on page 75.

Hint 31
Snow Fakes
This is the beginning and
ending of a route with a
score of 40.

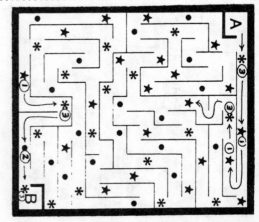

$16

$17

$23

$24

$39

$40

Solution 30
Cubistics

Three of the cubes could not have been made from the pattern. In number 2, the T should be rotated 90 degrees as shown. In number 6, the T should be an O. In number 7, the C is backwards.

71

33. FOOTSIE

If you can't bear the monotony of jogging, jumping rope, or swimming laps anymore, number the flagstones in your patio like this. Then start with any of the five boxes bordering the upper corner (numbers 1 to 5) and try to hop on one foot to HOME until you can do it by hopping on only ten different stones totaling fifty points, never moving diagonally. If you don't sprain an ankle, you should do it in two minutes. A hint appears on page 74 and a solution on page 77.

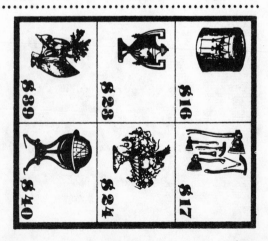

Hint 32
Tag Sale
Multiple quantities of only two of the items will give you a correct answer.

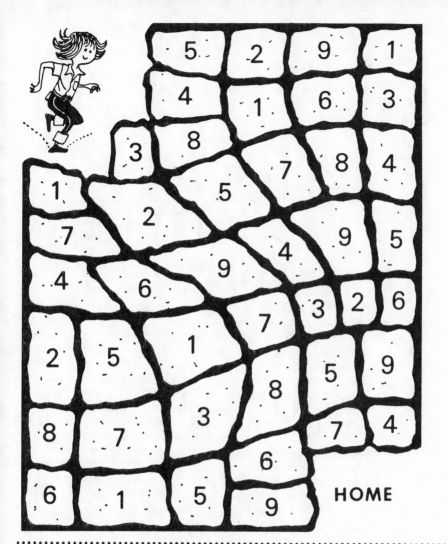

HOME

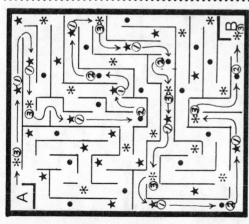

PAT-TURNS

34. THE SHATTERED URN

In the year 1664 A.D., three of the wisest advisers in the court of Emperor K'ang Hsi were summoned to inspect some broken pieces of pottery as you see them scattered here. The wise men were ordered, without touching the pieces, to predict the exact shape of the object these pieces would make when assembled. They then had to use their extrasensory perception to number the fragments so that their numbers would match those that the Emperor had arbitrarily assigned to each of the pieces on the drawing of the urn he had hidden in the sleeve of his robe. (You are more fortunate than the wise men, because we have shown you the Emperor's answer with each piece numbered and in place.) The Emperor condemned each man to one year of service as the court jester for each piece incorrectly numbered. Ten years is unthinkable; five years is horrible; two years is still pretty bad. A hint appears on page 76 and, if you can bear to look, a solution on page 79.

Hint 33
Footsie

These first two hops will start you on your way to a total of fifty points on ten stones, especially if the last stone equals the total of the first two.

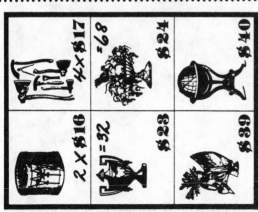

EYE-QUES

35. NOW DON'T GET MAD

Try your hand at organizing this confusion of numbers. You will find, right, three groups of numbers in random order. In which group — A, B, or C — should each of the numbers in the box at the top logically be placed? When you figure this out (in a blinding flash of rage and anguish), spring this on your worst enemy, your smartypants sister, or both. If your sister doesn't get it inside of two minutes, don't just stand there smirking, start running, because when she does, she'll be pretty angry. A hint appears on page 78 and a solution on page 81.

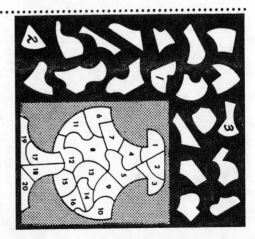

Hint 34
The Shattered Urn

The pieces are not always shown right side up. We have numbered a few to get you started.

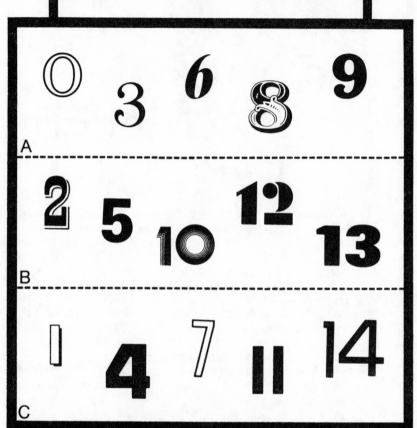

16 17 38

0 3 6 8 9

A

2 5 10 12 13

B

1 4 7 11 14

C

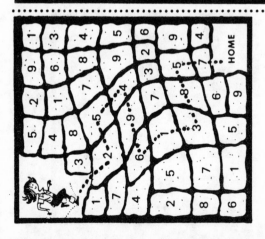

ROUTES

36. WACKO WALLPAPER CAPER

Some day, early in the morning, the San Andreas fault is going to open up under a house that has citron yellow, moss green, and teal blue wallpaper in the breakfast nook. That wallpaper will have a symmetrical, repeating pattern of a bird in a tree on a plain background. The quake will be so violent that it will shake the birds and trees apart and scatter them all over the background as you see them here. If the owners called you from your bed to help them start sorting out their wallpaper, could you draw just three straight lines (each going from one border of the wall area shown opposite to another) that would enclose both a bird and a tree within each area without touching any of them? If you keep calm and a helper holds the other end of the chalk line, you should be able to figure this one out in about eight minutes. A hint appears on page 80 and a solution on page 83.

Hint 35
Now Don't Get Mad

The numerical values are irrelevant. If you still have not arrived at a solution after figuring and figuring, sit down before you turn to page 81 where the solution appears.

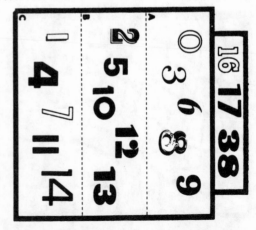

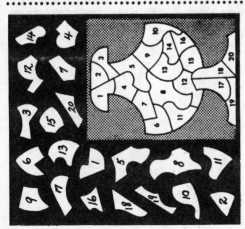

Solution 34
The Shattered Urn

PAT-TURNS

37. MATCHING MINOANS

When the Queen of ancient Crete had a garage sale in her palace at Knossos, she decided to part with six vases she and King Minos had received as wedding presents. The six vases *looked* alike, but were actually three identical pairs with slight differences. The Queen's three sisters wanted the vases, but since princesses turn up their royal noses at anything but perfectly matching crockery, they wouldn't buy them until they had figured out which were the pairs. The Queen was anxious to help, because she wanted the money to buy new curtains for the throne room. How quickly can you spot the matching Minoan vases? Par is about three minutes; less, if you have a keen eye for octopi. A hint appears on page 82 and a solution on page 85.

. . . .

Hint 36
Wacko Wallpaper
Caper
The lines just skin by the
heads, feet, and tails of
some of the birds shown
here where the arrows
point.

Solution 35
Now Don't Get Mad

The numbers in group A are all shapes with only *curves*. Group C has only *straight lines*. Group B contains *both* curved and straight lines. Sooooo, 38 belongs in group A; 16 in group B; and 17 in group C. Now calm *down*! Get a grip on yourself. You *promised* you wouldn't get mad.

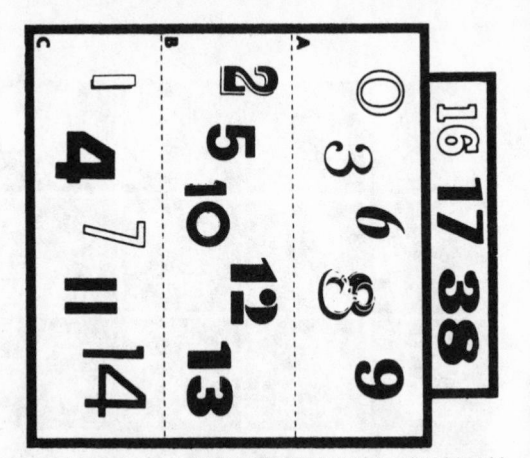

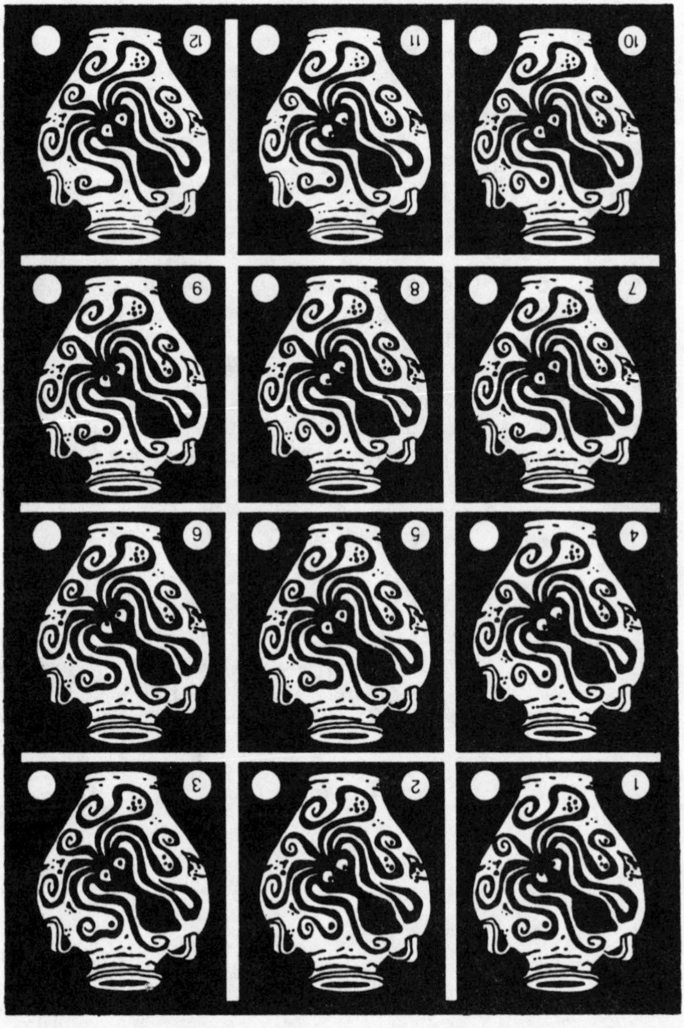

NIMBLE NUMBERS

38. WITCHES' TEST

Your grade school math teacher probably didn't tell you that witchcraft and mathematics are sister arts. This grid of twenty-five squares contains six of Hecate's symbols in place of numbers. By translating them into the numbers they stand for, the rows will add across and down to the totals shown at the right side and bottom. If you have to figure this out mathematically by trial and error, you probably are not a witch! A hint appears on page 84, a solution on page 87.

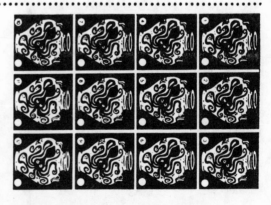

Hint 37
Matching Minoans
Note the eyes,
disappearing dots, and
which direction the
tentacles twist at the ends.

●	2	✳	2	○	22
6	✚	✖	★	✖	24
2	●	★	○	6	23
◉	✳	✖	★	2	22
✚	★	2	◉	✳	18
28	19	21	17	24	

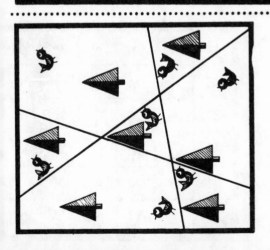

Solution 36
Wacko Wallpaper
Caper

ROUTES

39. BEAT THE BOBBIES

London had a great rise in crime in one of its large parks. But only four policemen could be assigned to the park to observe every path. Place Xs to represent the four bobbies at the four different points that permit them to look down every street in the park. Par is six minutes. A hint appears on page 86, a solution on page 89.

Hint 38
Witches' Test

The star is a one,
The circle a five.
If we tell you more
You needn't strive.

28	✚	⊙	2	6	●
19	★	✱	●	✚	2
21	2	✖	★	✖	✱
17	⊙	★	○	★	2
24	✱	2	6	✖	○
	18	22	23	24	22

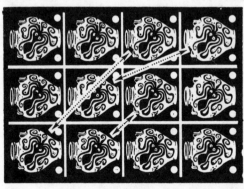

Solution 37
Matching Minoans

Numbers 1 and 9, 4 and 8,
5 and 12.

PAT-TURNS

40. FIND THE COMBO

How quickly can you find the number or letter that's to the right of a dot, above a star, below a 5, and to the left of an R? Circle the correct answer. Or, better still, leave it alone and see how long it takes someone else to find it. Start timing *after* he or she has read the above instructions through once carefully. Par is two minutes. A hint appears on page 88, a solution on page 91.

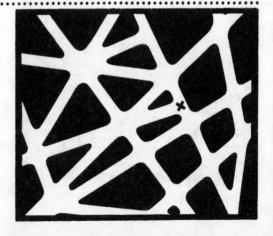

Hint 39
Beat the Bobbies
Wherever they station
themselves, the bobbies
will need 360-degree
vision, except for the one
spot we have shown here.

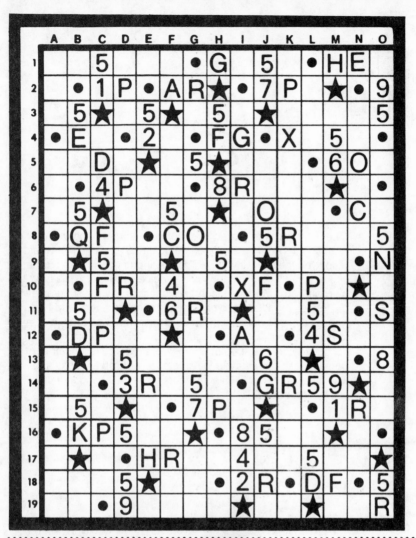

22	24	23	22	18	
5	7	6	2	4	24
2	1	5	1	8	17
4	7	1	7	2	21
2	3	9	4	1	19
9	6	2	8	3	28

Solution 38
Witches' Test

PAT-TURNS

41. DISS-PLAY

One night you were asked to decorate a store window in which craft objects from nine different Middle Eastern countries would be displayed the next day. (This has nothing to do with this puzzle, but you deserve to know that you have trained your pet koala bear to help with your window-decorating business. He is just completing the job for you.) Early the next morning the store received bad news. When the countries were told their work was to be displayed together, all but two of them backed out. You have only four minutes before the store opens. What is the smallest number of bars that can be removed to leave only two display areas and which bars are they? A hint appears on page 90 and a (tricky) solution on page 93.

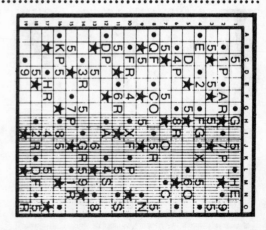

Hint 40
Find the Combo
The correct combo can
be found in the unshaded
half of the grid.

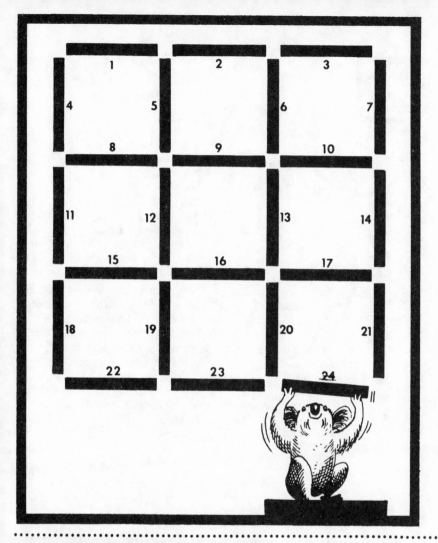

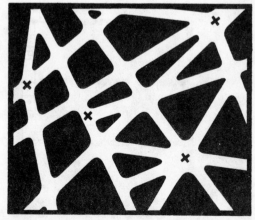

Solution 39
Beat the Bobbies

NIMBLE NUMBERS

42. CROSS NUMBERS

This is like a crossword puzzle with numbers. At the start of each horizontal or vertical row of boxes, a half-box with a number in it (the "clue") is attached to the top half or the bottom half of the first box. The top clue number shows the sum of the numbers to be filled into the boxes horizontally to the right. The lower clue number shows the sum of numbers to be filled in beneath it vertically. See the example in the upper boxes. Only the numbers 1 to 9 are used, and no number is repeated in any horizontal or vertical sequence. Frequently the numbers you fill in must work in both directions. The objective here is not speed — it's accuracy. A hint appears on page 92 and a solution on page 95.

Hint 41
Diss-Play
One country is about one ninth the size of the other, and the sum of the numbers of the bars on the sides of the smaller is exactly 50.

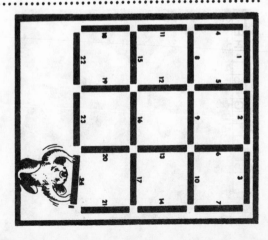

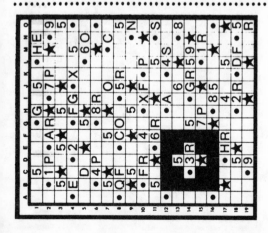

ROUTES

43.LONG SHORT CIRCUIT

What button do you press to light the bulb? Don't be shocked! There are a number of splices in the wires. You can follow a line in any direction where it crosses another. You will never have to retrace your path in the opposite direction on any segment of any line. You will do well to complete this maze in fewer than ten minutes. A hint appears on page 94. May you find a less tortuous route than our solution, which appears on page 97.

A hint appears on page 94.
our solution, which appears on page 97.

Hint 42
Cross Numbers
We have filled in the first few boxes to start you going. Once you get the hang, it goes faster.

Solution 41
Diss-Play

The smallest number of bars it is possible to remove is eight. They are: 5, 6, 8, 10, 15, 17, 19, and 20.

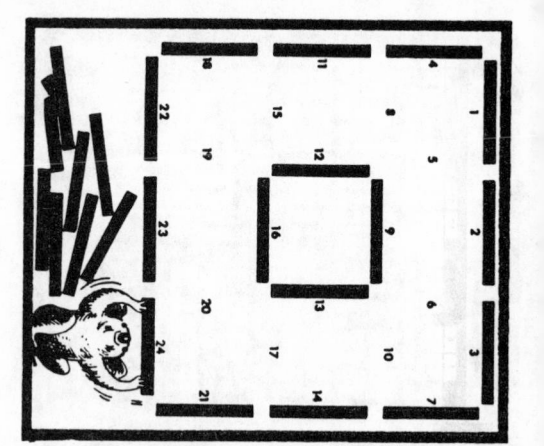

PAT-TURNS

44. COORDI-MATES

The nine boxed designs arranged around the top and right side of the picture match nine squares in the picture. Each square in the picture grid can be identified with a pair of numbers and a pair of letters. As you match each separate boxed design with the matching square in the picture, write its grid number and letter in the blank space next to it. Par is three minutes. A hint appears on page 96 and a solution on page 99.

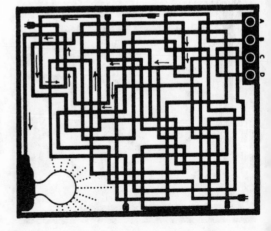

Hint 43
Long Short Circuit
If you are stuck, start with button C and follow it until you can pick up the route to the bulb marked with arrows here.

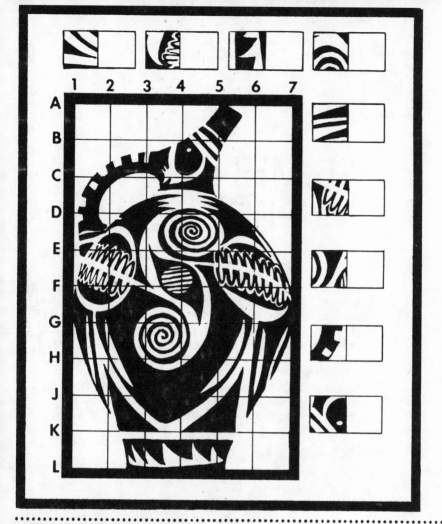

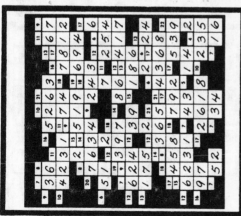

EYE-QUES

45. MENU, PLEASE

Five old friends had a reunion at their favorite restaurant. Each man ordered something to drink, an entree, and a dessert. John and Mr. Jackson had martinis and James and Mr. Jones ordered scotch. Mr. Jenkins had coke since he was driving. John and Mr. Jennings ordered steak. Joe and Mr. Jenkins had roast beef. For dessert, Joe and Mr. Jordan ate chocolate cake, while Jerry and Mr. Jenkins had pie. The other man had ice cream. No two men sitting next to each other were served two things the same. Who had pheasant and what did Jack eat? Par is five minutes. A hint appears on page 98 and a solution on page 101.

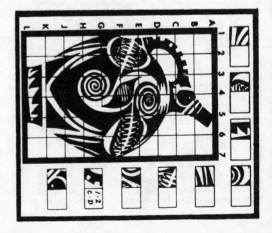

Hint 44
Coordimates

We have identified the correct location of one piece by writing its coordinates in the box next to it.

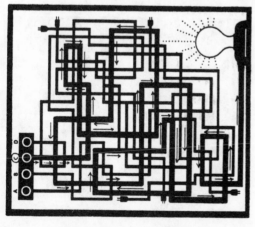

Solution 43
Long Short Circuit

NIMBLE NUMBERS

46. HARUM - SCOREM

These targets were tacked on a fence by a National Guard ordinance officer for future use. But a trigger-happy corporal took ten shots at them (shown by the black and white dots). Many shots went through more than one target. Counting all the holes in all the targets, what was the corporal's score? (He was docked one day's pay for each point and joined the Peace Corps.) A hint appears on page 100 and a solution on page 103.

Hint 45
Menu, Please
The location and name of each man has been given here.

ROUTES

47. THE VESPA VIRGIN

Giuseppe Colombo made his fortune in the U.S. by importing used Vespa motor scooters, converting them for amphibious use, and selling them to hapless purchasers of valueless swampland in Florida. He then returned to his native Rome to find a wife. He was properly introduced to his father's neighbor's innocent daughter and asked for her hand in marriage on the condition that she would first accompany him on a trip during which she must prove her moral purity by refusing his advances. He marked his map with black dots at the most beautiful spots where they might be tempted to linger. He laid out his route to avoid them but to cross each segment of the map's outlines *between* the dots once and only once, and only in connected *straight* lines, starting at Rome, ending at Geneva. As you see, there are twenty-one segments. What is the least number of connected straight lines you can draw, within the white area in and around the map, to make a route that will pass through each of the segments once? Twelve lines is *intelligentissimo*; fifteen is *molto buono*; eighteen is A-OK. A hint appears on page 102. Giuseppe's solution is shown on page 105.

● ●

Hint 46
Harum-Scorem

The holes in target B hit the bull's-eye (25) in target C, 10 in D, and 5 in A. The total score on target E is 50 points; see 'em?

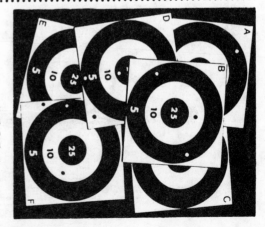

Solution 45
Menu, Please

1. Joe Jackson had a martini, roast beef, and cake.
2. Jerry Jones had scotch, pheasant, and cheese pie.
3. John Jordan had a martini, steak, and cake.
4. Jack Jenkins had a coke, roast beef, and pie.
5. James Jennings had scotch, steak, and ice cream.

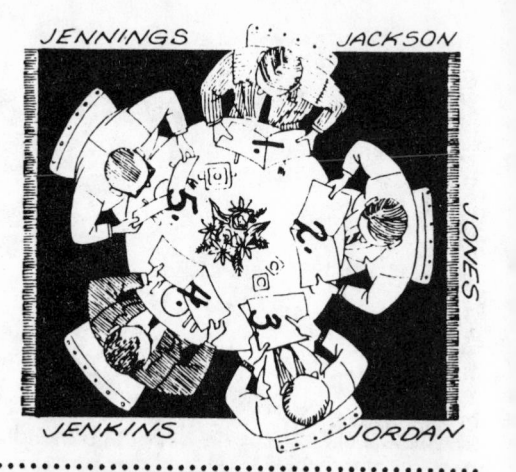

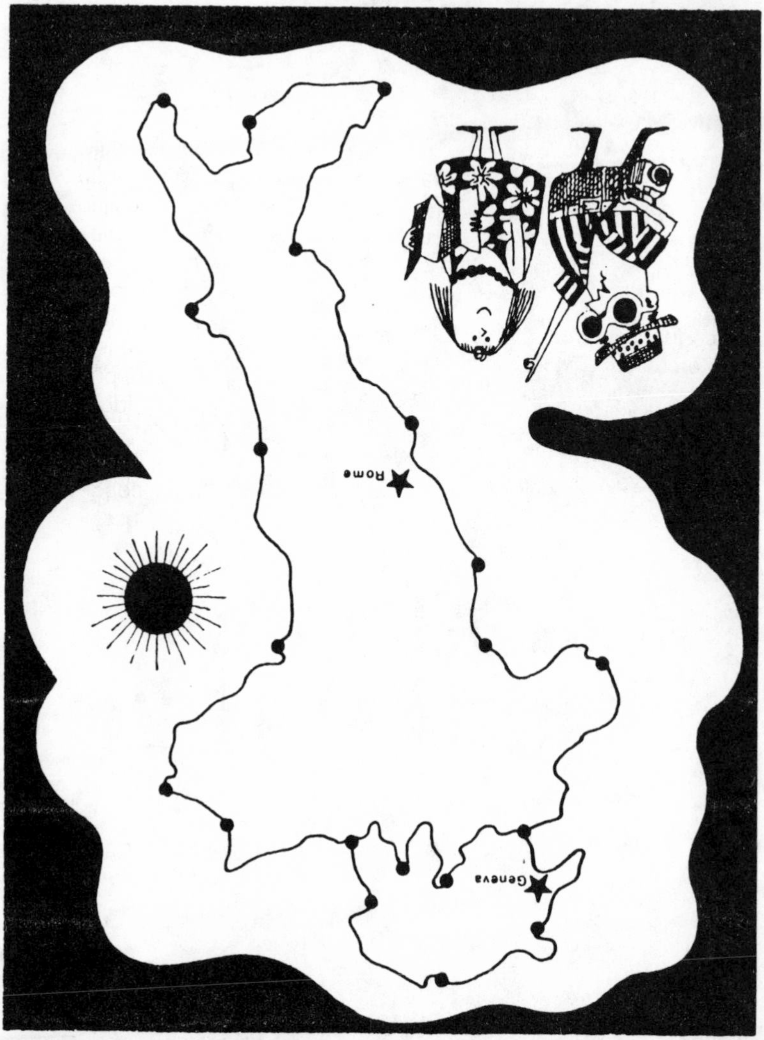

48. ROYAL DIVORCE

Rearrange these sixteen playing cards so that no two of the same value or the same suit are in the same row either vertically, horizontally, or diagonally. If you don't want to cut the cards out, write in the cards' initials (JH for jack of hearts, QS for queen of spades, etc.) in the small boxes. It should not take you more than five minutes to break up these happy marriages. A hint appears on page 104 and a solution on page 107.

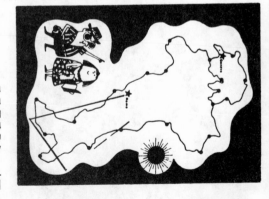

Hint 47
The Vespa Virgin
As you see here, one line may pass through more than one segment. We have drawn in the first three lines of Giuseppe's twelve-line solution.

Solution 46
Harum-Scorem

Target A: 5+5+5   =15
Target B: 10+5+5   =20
Target C: 25+5   =30
Target D: 10+25+5   =40
Target E:
  5+5+5+10+25   =50
Target F: 5+5+10   =20
                  ——
Total score   175

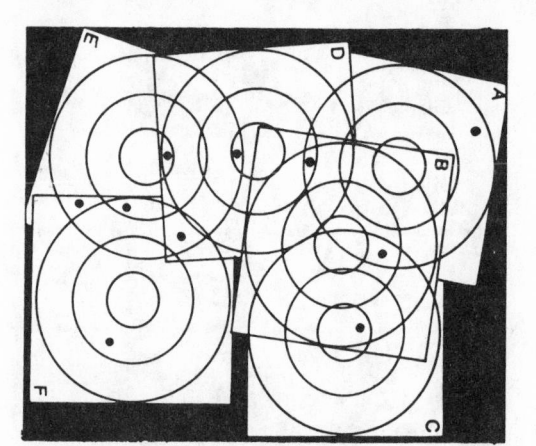

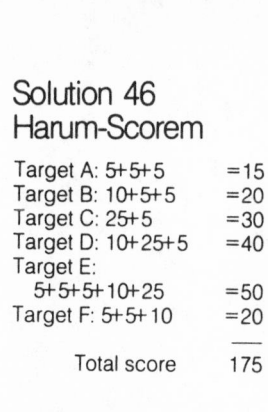

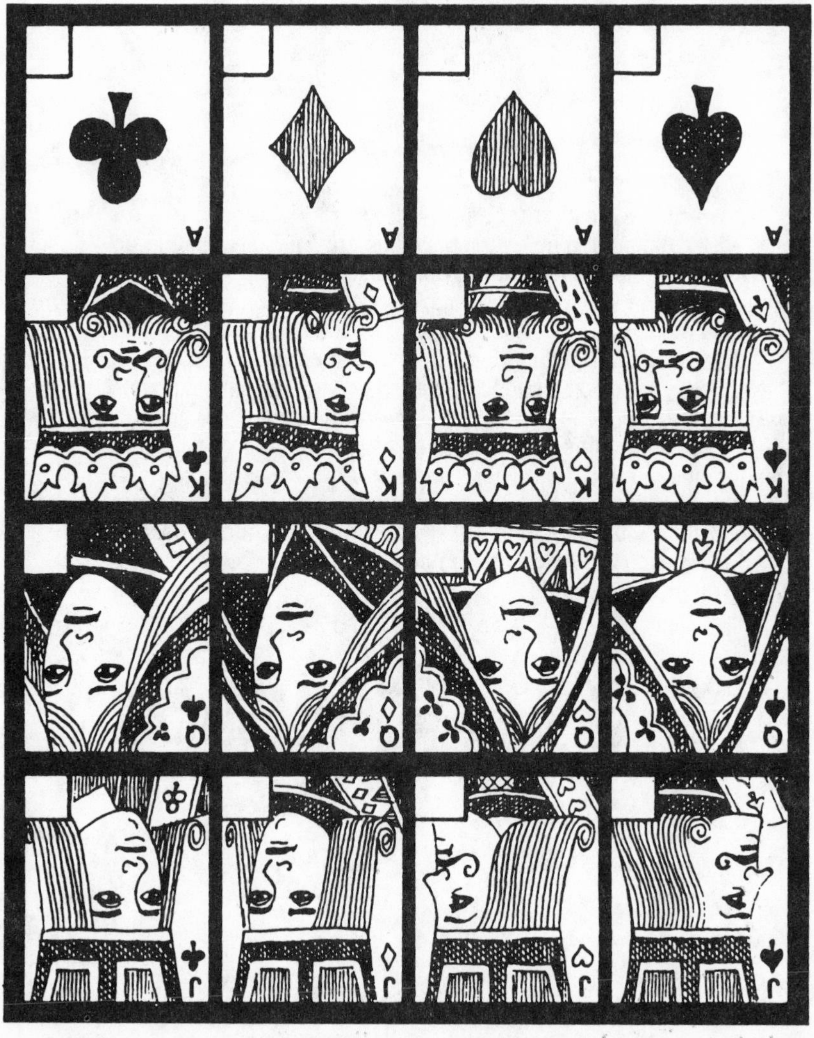

EYE-QUES

49. BIRDS' CALL

It takes some ingenuity to bring up a bird if one is not a bird oneself — and the same species to boot. So when a zoo breaks up and offers its collection of live birds to the public, it should test each prospective owner. Suppose, for example, you wanted the giant five-foot-tall Australian cassowary (the star) out of this collection of thirteen rara avises perched in a circle. To qualify, first you must eliminate all the birds by counting clockwise from any one of them and counting out the thirteenth. (The koala bear in the middle doesn't count.) Start counting over again from the next bird in the circle, count around the remaining birds, and count out the thirteenth bird again. Keep doing this until only the bird of your dreams remains. If you can pull that off, you get the bird, as it were. A hint appears on page 106 and a solution on page 109.

Hint 48
Royal Divorce
We have relocated four of
the cards into the corners
as they appear in the
solution.

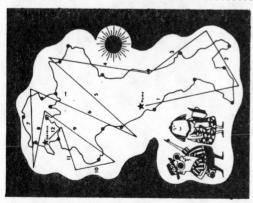

PAT-TURNS

50. TIME SIGNS

A gas main exploded under a typewriter factory with such force that it blew the room where all the symbols were stored into orbit. Astronomers on a planet named Htrae, which is located in an as-yet-undiscovered black hole named Tsap, got all excited when they noticed a predictable pattern developing in these eight radio telescope photos they took each morning for a week and a day. They offered a brimming glass of freshly distilled "emit" to the citizen who could correctly predict the pattern on the ninth day. You have only two light-years to solve this one. After that the prize will spin backward in time too far to reach. A hint appears on page 108 and a solution on page 111.

Hint 49
Birds' Call
Do not start counting at or near the cassowary (starred). (For one thing, you could get a nasty bump on the head from the bump on his head.) Keep as far away from that old Aussie as you can.

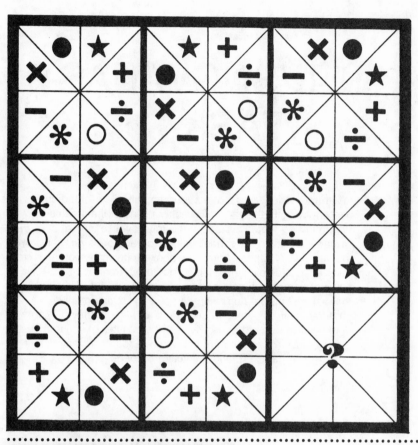

ROUTES

51.'SNOW EASY TASK

Year ago, four students at a suburban school for gifted children were playing in the snow after school. One of them came up with the following idea. "Let's all stand in a row like this (a, b, c, d), with our backs to the school wall, then each of us run to his own home (A, B, C, D). But here's the hook. If anyone's footprints cross over anyone else's before we all get to our front doors (Xs), we all have to come back here and try again." They did it with only one false start, but don't worry if you can't. None of these children ever amounted to much in later life, but they did jog a lot and lived to ripe old ages. Par is three minutes, if you *don't* use a pencil. Just in case you are not gifted in the same way, a hint appears on page 110 and a solution on page 113.

Hint 50
Time Signs
Notice that the symbols
always appear in the same
sequence within each
picture. Now, if you were
to rotate them . . .

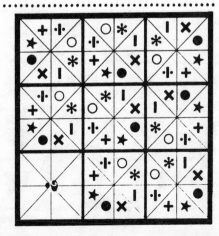

Solution 49
Birds' Call

We have numbered all the birds, with the cassowary as number 8. Start counting with the bird marked number 1 and follow the instructions — if you want to end up with a five-foot Australian cassowary, that is.

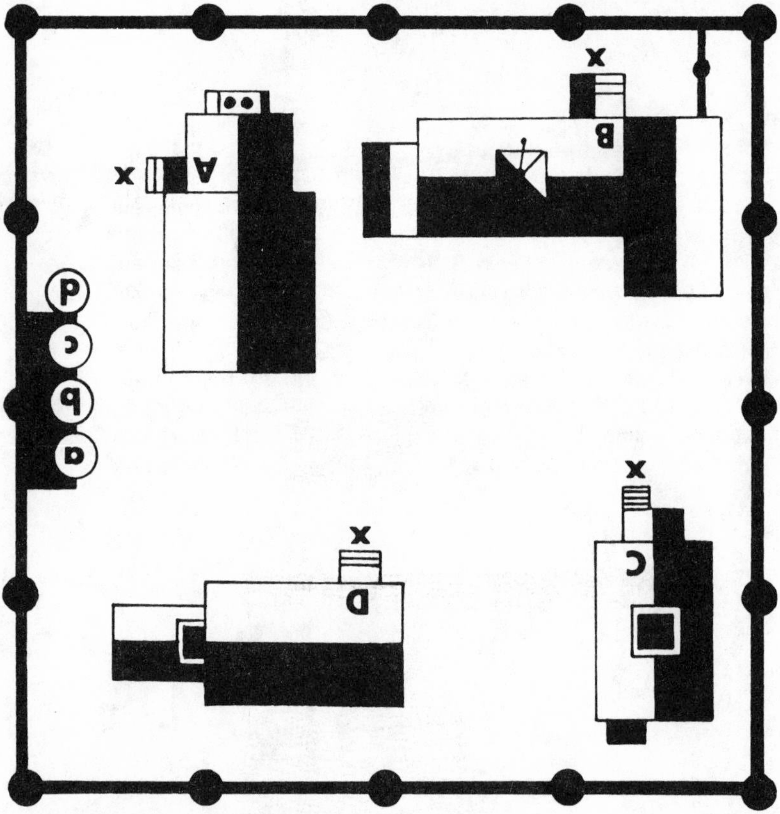

NIMBLE NUMBERS

52. CAN WILLIAM TELL?

After William shot the apple off his son's head he got to be a bit of a show-off — forever shooting the feathers out of people's caps and flagons out of their hands. So the townspeople set up this target to keep him out of their hair for awhile. They told him it wasn't enough just to hit the periods on the question marks. First he must tell them what number logically should be in that space each time. If you happen to see poor William still standing there leaning on his bow and squinting at this target, tell him that he doesn't have to do it by trial and error. There is a logical system to it. You get to put the apple on top of *your* head if it takes you more than two and a half minutes to figure this out. A hint appears on page 112 and a solution on page 115.

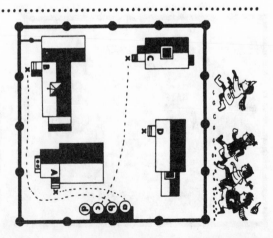

Hint 51
'Snow Easy Task'
Students a and b tried to
go the easy way. But this
meant that c would have to
cross over their footprints
to get home. So they had
to return and start over
again.

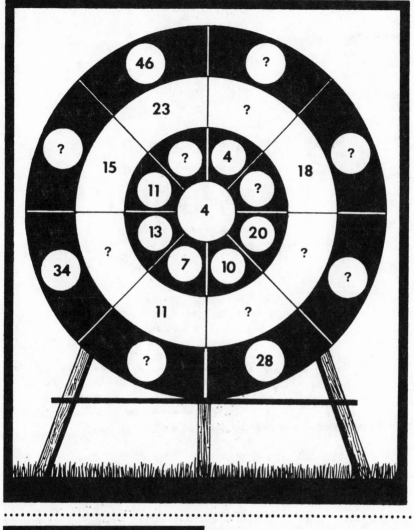

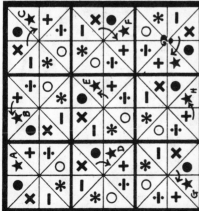

Solution 50
Time Signs

Starting at the upper left and moving horizontally, you'll find a three-step sequence: one move counter-clockwise, two moves clockwise. The sequence is repeated, eventually giving you the correct pattern for the ninth day.

111

53. SALLY'S EXPENSIVE FRIENDS

On Sundays, Sally drives to town to visit friends. She always stays too long at each house and gets a parking ticket. They range in cost from $1 to $7 (see numbers). Whenever she gets a ticket, she hops directly over to visit someone in another part of town where a ticket costs exactly the same. She thinks that she won't stay too long there, therefore the money she saves by not getting *that* ticket will pay for the one she just got — making her even. Sally always enters town at the top arrow and leaves at the bottom arrow. What is the sequence of numbers that will produce the lowest total of fines? Remember, she drives to one number, hops to its twin, drives to another, hops to *its* twin, and so on, until she comes to a route that leads out of town. She does not need to visit all her friends. It will cost her more than $30 and less than $40. Par is five minutes. A hint appears on page 114 and a solution on page 117.

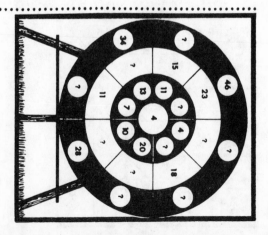

Hint 52
Can William Tell?
Did you notice that
7 + 4 = 11?
And that twice 23 = 46?
Heavy input!

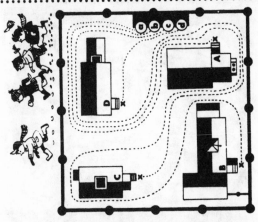

Solution 51
'Snow Easy Task'

NIMBLE NUMBERS

54. EQUAL TIME

In each of the four problems at right you are to place the numbers at the left in the boxes with the dark outlines. The math signs must be placed between these boxes. When the numbers and math signs are correctly placed, as shown by that smart-aleck koala bear in the example at the top, an equation will be formed in each row. Use each number and sign shown. Par is seven minutes. A hint appears on page 116 and a solution on page 119.

Hint 53
Sally's Expensive Friends

The second number is double the first, the fourth is double the third, the fifth (and last) is the sum of the second and third. Some hint. ⌀ ¿ ! #

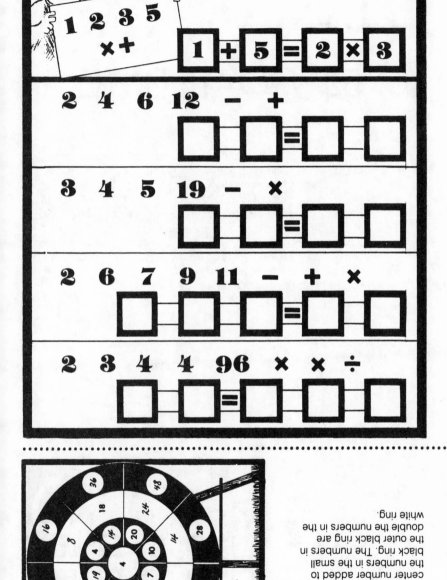

Solution 52
Can William Tell?

The numbers in the white ring are the totals of the center number added to the numbers in the small black ring. The numbers in the outer black ring are double the numbers in the white ring.

 ROUTES

55. ROAD BIKE

Luck played a key role in the first international bike race through the streets of Paris, held after World War II. The one stipulation was that the racers had to make the finish line in an even number of stops (each large dot is a stop) and not make the same stop twice. The winner, a fifty-three-year-old Bulgarian refugee riding a 1951 Harley, made it in eighteen stops, counting the finish. In three and a half minutes or less, can you find the route he followed? If you find a shorter route, you are obviously a spy trying to come in from the cold and are disqualified!!! A hint appears mysteriously on page 118 and a solution on page 121.

Hint 54

Equal Time

Don't assume that the sequence of the numbers or math signs means anything. The last number that has one. If the numbers are arranged that way, the first number in each row could be as shown.

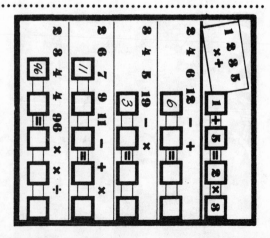

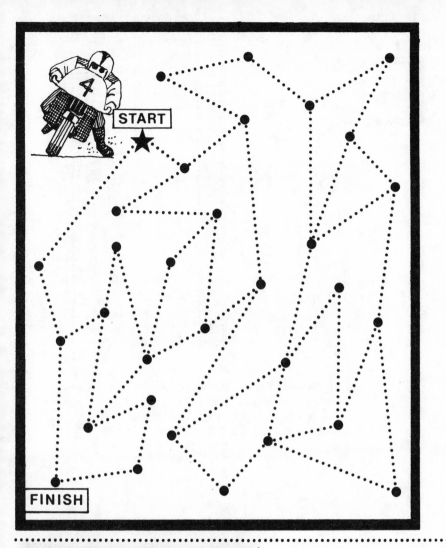

START

FINISH

NIMBLE NUMBERS

56. SNEAK - QUENCES

Fill in the empty boxes with the correct numbers to complete each sequence using the numbers already there. The numbers in each sequence always either increase or decrease the same amount from left to right or top to bottom. See the two examples at the top left. Once you figure out how to calculate the key number to add to or subtract from the number in each box, this puzzle goes very quickly, provided your arithmetic is accurate. If you make a mistake, it will show up right away because the numbers interlock in the same way the letters of words do in a crossword puzzle. If you haven't started completing any sequences within three minutes, turn to page 120 where you will find a hint to get you started. A complete solution is on page 123.

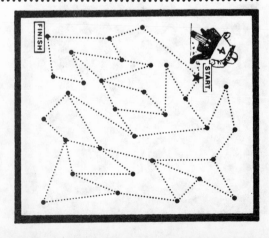

Hint 55
Road Bike
The winner, being
Bulgarian, naturally bore
off to his left at the start
and, having just escaped
across country, kept to the
outside of town as long as
he could (eight stops).

118

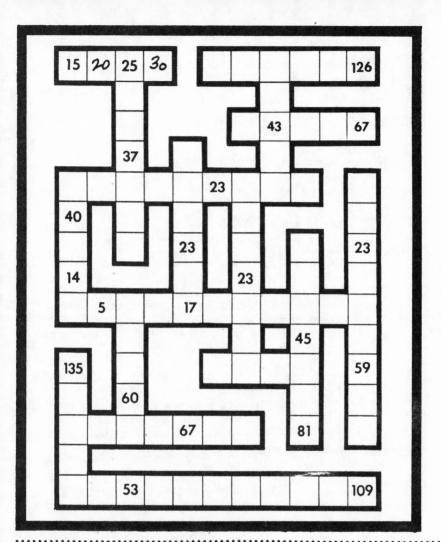

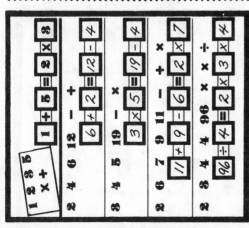

Solution 54
Equal Time

ROUTES

57. SYMBOL MAZEY MADNESS

Brace yourself! Each symbol allows you to jump a specific number of boxes (see legend). Search for the shortest route that will land you exactly on the circle at the bottom. To start, pick one of the symbols in the first five boxes in the upper-left corner of the grid. Some are shaded as an example of what would happen if you chose to start with the square symbol (4). The first move, which must always be downward, would land you four boxes below the square, on a triangle (3). From there on you may travel either horizontally or vertically. If any of these alternative moves lands you on a symbol, you may then move the number of boxes (three, in this case) indicated by the symbol you have just landed on. You may reverse direction but you may not cross over your own path already traveled on that route. There is one route with seventeen moves totaling fifty-four points. If you find it in four minutes you are doing well. (If you can even remember the *instructions* in four minutes, you're pretty good.) A hint appears on page 122 and a solution on page 125.

Hint 56
Sneak-Quences

Find a row or column with two numbers in it, and subtract one from the other. Count the number of boxes between them and add one. Divide that number into the difference between the two numbers printed in that row or column. Add or subtract that key number each time to fill the boxes in between.

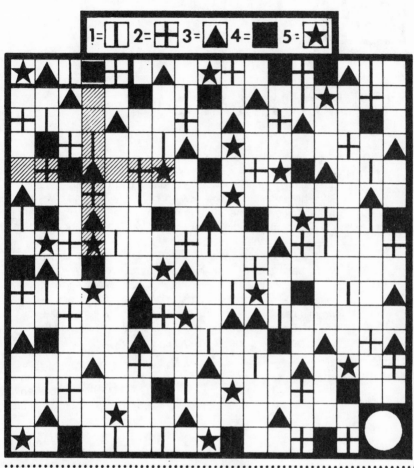

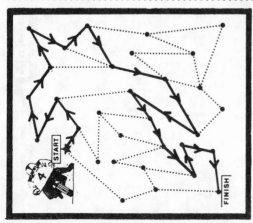

Solution 55
Road Bike

 PAT-TURNS

58. NUTS!

Ivan the Mad Inventor built a cabinet with eighty compartments to store the nine items he would need to repair his weird machines. Since his inventions never worked anyway, he whiled away his time by arranging the nine items so no item was in line with any other one horizontally, vertically, or diagonally. One day, though, he had to use three of the items to repair his 1941 Studebaker. Later, he replaced those items in *different* compartments that are shown empty here, but still in such a way that none of them was in line with each other or any of the other six items. What three items did he relocate in which three empty compartments? It took him only two minutes — but then, he was slightly crazy. It may take you longer. (So what does that make *you* if you do it in *less* time?) A hint appears on page 124 and a solution on page 127.

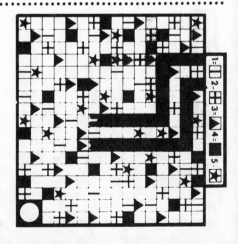

Hint 57
Symbol Mazey
Madness
We have started you on
the correct route, which
begins at the plus sign.

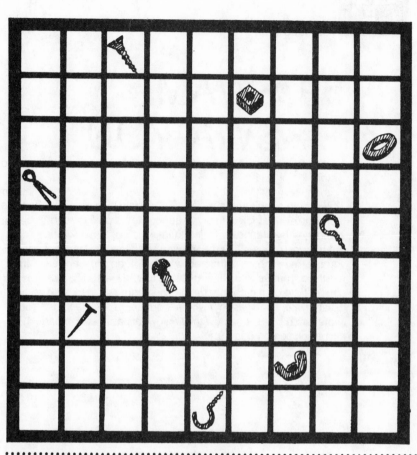

EYE-QUES

59. SWAMI SWA-YOU

This is both a trick and a puzzle. The puzzle is to figure out how the trick works. The trick is that you appear to be able to read someone else's mind by telling them which of these symbols they are thinking of. Ask the other person to choose any symbol and tell you only in which rows (numbers 1, 2, 3, 4, and 5) it appears. If, for example, you are told, "It appears in rows 2, 4, and 5," you concentrate on the chart for a few moments and then, with an air of great mystery and wisdom, you announce, "You selected the star in the circle." A hint on how this trick works appears on page 126 and a solution on page 9.

• •

Hint 58
Nuts!
You have already noticed that if you move one object, that usually forces you to move another. Well, all we will tell you is that he did *not* move either of the cup hooks or either of the nuts.

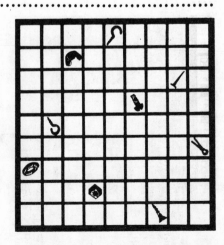

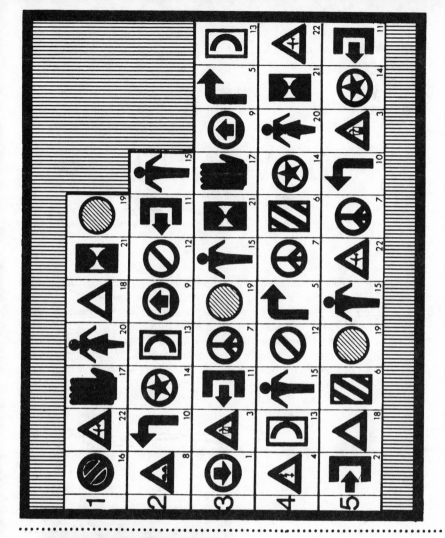

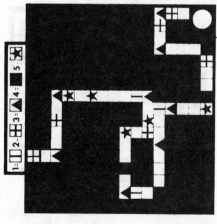

Solution 57
Symbol Mazey
Madness

125

PAT-TURNS

60. WHAT'S THE DIFFERENCE?

A counterfeit-bill engraver tried to make a copy of the Victorian vase engraving shown on the left, while he was serving time for being caught with the plates for a $10 bill with a perfect likeness of Madame Curie on it. Although he had plenty of time to do the job, he made eleven mistakes. As you find each of these differences between the two pictures, circle it. Par: ten to eleven, excellent; seven to nine, good; five to six, fair. A hint appears on page 8 and a solution on page 11.

Hint 59
Swami Swa-You

Have you noticed the small numbers in the squares with each symbol? The ones at the end of the rows nearest the large row numbers are the most important.

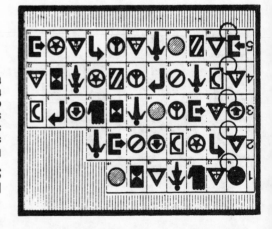

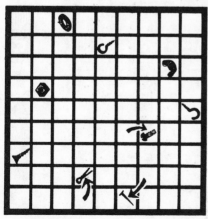

Solution 58
Nuts!

SYMBOL INDEX